ADVANCE PRAISE FOR

The Politics of Mercy
Catholic Life in an Era of Inequality, Racism, and Violence

"Yves Congar, the great French Dominican theologian, argued that a tradition can only survive into the next generation if the present one appropriates it and makes it its own. In their transformative work, Matthew T. Eggemeier and Peter Joseph Fritz propose the long-standing works of mercy as a **politics** constituted by spiritual practices, charitable works and structural change. This fully integrated, embodied, and practical twenty-first century model is a spectacular development for the future of the most ancient Christian forms of life, mercy. Read the book so as to live the politics, a very Catholic way of life."

—JAMES F. KEENAN, S.J.
CANISIUS PROFESSOR, BOSTON COLLEGE

"With scholarly depth and intelligent writing, Eggemeier and Fritz offer readers an engaging and lucid foundation in Catholic Social Teaching while demonstrating its enduring relevance for our time. *The Politics of Mercy* is an important resource for university classrooms, parish formation programs, and anybody who is looking for an instructive and engaging book on how to think about and respond to some of the most pressing issues of our day—inequality, racism, and violence—from a Catholic Christian perspective."

— DANIEL P. HORAN, OFM, DUNS SCOTUS CHAIR IN SPIRITUALITY
CATHOLIC THEOLOGICAL UNION

"Refined in the classroom, this volume invites us to consider the virtue of mercy as integrally implicated in leading a full Christian life. I can easily imagine this book as a core text for adult discussion in a parish or as a college text. Highly recommended towards that end or for personal spiritual reading."

—LAWRENCE CUNNINGHAM
PROFESSOR EMERITUS, THE UNIVERSITY OF NOTRE DAME

The Politics of Mercy

The Politics of Mercy

Catholic Life in an Era of Inequality, Racism, and Violence

MATTHEW T. EGGEMEIER
and
PETER JOSEPH FRITZ

A HERDER & HERDER BOOK
THE CROSSROAD PUBLISHING COMPANY
NEW YORK

A Herder & Herder Book
The Crossroad Publishing Company www.crossroadpublishing.com

© 2020 by Matthew T. Eggemeier and Peter Joseph Fritz

The text of this book is set in 12/14 Filosofia OT.

Composition by Sophie Appel
Cover design by Sophie Appel
Cover artwork by Peter Joseph Fritz

Library of Congress Cataloging-in-Publication Data
available upon request from the Library of Congress.
ISBN 978-0-8245-9809-9 paperback
ISBN 978-0-8245-0186-0 cloth
ISBN 978-0-8245-0188-4 ePub
ISBN 978-0-8245-0194-5 mobi

Books published by The Crossroad Publishing Company may be purchased at special quantity discount rates for classes and institutional use. For information, please e-mail sales@crossroadpublishing.com.

To our students
at the
College of the Holy Cross

CONTENTS

ACKNOWLEDGMENTS

THIS BOOK BEGAN WITH three team-taught courses in the Department of Religious Studies at the College of the Holy Cross. Thank you to our department chair, William Reiser, SJ, for supporting this venture. Thanks also to all of our colleagues in Religious Studies and beyond at the College. Thank you to President Philip Boroughs, SJ, and Provost Margaret Freije for their support for our scholarship at the College. Each of us received Research and Publication funding through the Committee on Faculty Scholarship and the Office of the Provost and Dean of the College for research that went into this book. We are grateful for this. Thanks, too, to Stacy Riseman and Rachel Girardi for all the work they do to facilitate and to foster our scholarship.

This book has a longer, more specialized companion text, *Send Lazarus: Catholicism and the Crises of Neoliberalism* (Fordham University Press, 2020). Portions of *Send Lazarus*, Chapters 3 and 5, were adapted to provide some of the content in this one. Thank you to Fred Nachbaur, Director of Fordham University Press, and to the press for permitting this adaptation.

Special thanks are due to Chris Myers, Senior Editor at Crossroad, for the extended conversation—which began over what would become *Send Lazarus*—that led to the composition of *The Politics of Mercy*. Thanks to Daniel Castillo and Andrew Prevot for putting us in initial contact with Chris. Thanks also to Gwendolyn Herder, Julie Boddorf, and all others involved in bringing it to print.

We would like to thank Eric and Colleen Fitts and everyone else at Bethlehem Farm; Aloysious Mowe, SJ, Cindy Bomben, and Arnout Mertens at the Jesuit Refugee Service International Office in Rome, Italy; and Chris and Jackie Allen-Douçot at the Hartford Catholic Worker for their hospitality and for sharing their work with us so that we may share it with others.

Also deserving of thanks are Alice Cheng; Tom and Judy Eggemeier; Chris, Sara, Jonah, and Bea Eggemeier; Tom, Katie, Libby, and Will

Eggemeier; Matt and Paula Fritz; Dixie Rokusek; Rochelle Fritz; Zephaniah, Gideon, Beatrice, and Malachi Fritz; and all of our students at the College of the Holy Cross, to whom this book is dedicated.

T HE FOLLOWING OFFICIAL CATHOLIC Church documents play an important role in this book. We cite them within our text in parentheses,
as is common practice in writings on Catholic social thought. Here are
the abbreviations we use in those citations.

CC   *Catechism of the Catholic Church* (1992) – John Paul II
            (promulgated)
CS   *The Compendium of the Social Doctrine of the Catholic Church*
            (2004) – Pontifical Council for Justice and Peace
CV   *Caritas in Veritate* (2009) – Benedict XVI
DC   *Deus Caritas Est* (2005) – Benedict XVI
EG   *Evangelii Gaudium* (2013) – Francis
EV   *Evangelium Vitae* (1995) – John Paul II
GS   *Gaudium et Spes* (1965) – Second Vatican Council
LE   *Laborem Exercens* (1981) – John Paul II
LS   *Laudato Si'* (2015) – Francis
OW   *Open Wide Our Hearts* (2018) – United States Conference of
            Catholic Bishops
PP   *Populorum Progressio* (1967) – Paul VI
PT   *Pacem in Terris* (1963) – John XXIII

All references to the Bible, unless otherwise indicated, are taken from
the New American Bible (NAB), the translation used in the worship
and prayer of U.S. Catholics. The NAB is accessible online through the
United States Conference of Catholic Bishops website: http://usccb.
org/bible/index.cfm. We ask that the reader have the Bible handy
while reading this book as an aid in following along with our biblical
references.

A T THE OUTSET, WE want to articulate this book's thesis and its distinctive argumentative approach. First, the thesis: Catholic life in an era of inequality, racism, and violence should reimagine the traditional works of mercy as a politics that entails spiritual practices, direct action or charitable work, and long-term structural transformation or justice. Next, the argument: the distinctiveness of this project is twofold. We treat five pressing social crises (inequality, migration, mass incarceration, war, and climate change) as interconnected, and we argue that the works of mercy reimagined as a politics of mercy are particularly well suited to addressing these interconnected crises.

We decided to write this book because of our shared commitment to social justice, which derives from our commitment as theologians, teachers, and people of faith to the Catholic Church and its stated mission of mercy. The summer of 2018, with its revelations of continued and entrenched sexual abuse in the U.S. Catholic Church, caused us to rethink what's involved in writing a book like this. The moral and religious authority of the Catholic Church—especially with regard to mercy— has collapsed as a result of the ongoing sex-abuse crisis. If Catholics are going to remain Catholic, or explain to others why they are going to remain Catholic (let alone why others should *become* Catholic!), they need to be able to point to the moral and theological resources that remain in the Catholic tradition despite the church's institutional failures. Put otherwise, we need fresh **apologetics** for the continued relevance of the Catholic Church in the United States of America and beyond. We seek to offer here one way of explaining the faith to people skeptical of it, and deepening the life of faith for those who hold it. We do so through the prism of the vision of mercy articulated by Pope Francis and embodied by several Catholic communities and organizations. While the church and its representatives have sinned, and much of its institutional authority has been lost, Catholics at the grassroots level continue to live out the gospel message in a vibrant and often radical way.

We originally intended to assist the Catholic faithful in seeing the interconnectedness of the Catholic Church's mission with some—and we do emphasize only *some*—of the most pressing social crises of our time, and to convince our fellow Catholics that they should work to address these crises. In our time, significant segments of the Catholic population espouse something akin to the prosperity gospel, deny climate change, believe patriotism involves support for endless war, and are adamant in their disdain for migrants and the incarcerated, or at least align themselves with politicians who are. This cannot stand. We are faced, though, with the problem that the U.S. Catholic hierarchy's focus has been placed on sexual issues, and the hierarchy and some Catholic media outlets have lent support to politicians who hold that critiques of the dominant social order (with its tendencies toward inequality, racism, and political violence) are signs of a partisan, anti-American ideology. In the midst of this complex, polarized political situation, there is no easy way to reclaim the priority of Catholic identity over political affiliation. But we see it as urgent to advocate for a holistic vision of Catholic life centered on mercy. From this central point, all other relations (including party loyalty) should be drawn. Now is a critical time for theologians like us to join the call of activists, organizers, and other faithful people at the grassroots level to call the church back to what should always be regarded as its chief mission: to proclaim, as much through action as word, the good news of God's mercy.

This book joins other efforts to restore the moral authority of the church as the people of God. It does this by applying Catholic social thought (we'll define this term shortly) to today's world situation, marked as it is by extreme economic inequality, systemic racism, militarism, and disdain for ecosystems of all sorts. The Catholic Church, when it is doing what it is supposed to be doing, is distinctively situated to discover connections between the various crises that threaten people and all of God's creation today, given Christian teachings on the goodness of creation, the dignity of every human person, and the injunction to be merciful as God is merciful (Lk 6:36). We aim in this book to help you understand these resources, and how they're being enacted by specific Catholic organizations and communities. Even further, if this book helps you to understand what's going on, to judge the crises as unacceptable and the Catholic action to address them as desirable, we hope that this understanding and this judgment will impel you to act.

If we plan to apply the moral authority and resources of the church to problems of this world, what exactly do we have in mind? While we engage the negative aspects of five pressing social crises, the motivation for doing this is that a Catholic vision for life is positive and hopeful. Our criticism of these crises comes from a standpoint of hope. We have positive reasons for foregrounding mercy insofar as we seek to build the abundant life that Jesus preached and lived (see Jn 10:10). In order to build that life, we must face honestly the way in which sin in the world undermines a Catholic vision for life.

To live an authentic Catholic life in the twenty-first century necessitates that we grapple with the crises of inequality, racism, and violence. Furthermore, it necessitates that we see these crises as interconnected; as Pope Francis says repeatedly in *Laudato Si'* (2015), "everything is connected." Pope Francis made this claim in the midst of his examination of the environmental crisis we now face. But he was careful to connect this crisis to other crises such as poverty, migration, and resource conflict. His point is that if we want environmental justice, we need simultaneously to uplift the poor, to seek justice for migrants and refugees, and to work for peace and reconciliation in the world.

We have organized the five crises examined in this book around the broader categories of inequality, racism, and violence.

Inequality: Pope Francis has argued that inequality is the root of all social evil. We treat it first because we want to take this claim seriously. In Chapter 1, we analyze wealth and poverty and focus on the precariousness of life for most people in the world as it contrasts with the concentration of wealth among the richest few.

Racism: Chapters 2 and 3 are organized under the category of **racism**, or assigning different value to people on the basis of their skin pigmentation. In Chapter 2, we explore the history of racialized exclusion as it relates to migration. Our particular focus is on the United States and the threat of mass deportation. In Chapter 3, we discuss racialized exclusion as it relates to imprisonment. We focus here, too, on the United States and the phenomenon of mass incarceration. In both chapters, we explore the ways in which the expulsion of people to the margins of society has served as a dominant way of dealing with racial difference in American history.

Violence: Chapters 4 and 5 are organized under the category of **violence**, or the use of force (in word or deed) to inflict harm. In

Chapter 4, we examine the violence perpetrated in war. In particular, we focus on American militarism as a potent manifestation of political violence. Chapter 5 explores the violence of environmental destruction as manifest not only in climate change, but also in its intersection with the four other pressing social crises we considered in prior chapters.

Our main vehicle for presenting mercy, the heart of the Catholic message, is modern **Catholic social thought**, a venerable tradition that spans more than 125 years. Catholic social thought reflects on questions of how people are to live properly with one another from the perspective of the Catholic faith. Catholic social thought emerges out of a long tradition of this type of reflection that is found in the scriptures (Hebrew prophets, the Gospels, Acts of the Apostles, the Letter of James), the early church (the Cappadocians, John Chrysostom, Augustine, Benedictine hospitality), the medieval church (mendicant orders and care for the poor), and the early modern church (like papal condemnations of slavery from Paul III's *Sublimis Deus* [1537] through Gregory XVI's *In Supremo* [1839]).

Within the broader category of Catholic social thought, and in many respects driving this trajectory of discourse, is **Catholic social teaching**. This phrase designates official, magisterial teachings by popes, bishops, and other church leaders tasked with making pronouncements on faith and morals. This teaching is often expressed in **encyclicals** (literally "circular letters") written by popes to be circulated to the whole church to offer reflection on an important theological, moral, or ethical matter. The modern encyclical tradition began with Pope Leo XIII's publication of *Rerum Novarum* (1891), on the relationship between capital and labor and the Catholic critique of socialism. This encyclical tradition was developed by subsequent popes, and has been supplemented by more occasional pieces, such as homilies, reflections, and messages. Local groups of bishops, including the United States Conference of Catholic Bishops, have also offered similar social writings and statements.

In this book, we use the method employed by the popes without constantly referencing specific encyclicals. We do invoke the writings and speeches of popes (particularly Pope Francis and Pope Benedict XVI), but we view our task as carrying forward the theological insights of the encyclical tradition and applying them to today's problems. Thus, in each chapter under "Catholic Social Thought," we reflect on a central theological idea that expresses the faith and moral commitments of the Catholic tradition: the human person's having been created as *imago Dei*/image of God (inequality), God's accompaniment of people (migration), the Paschal Mystery of Jesus Christ's suffering, death, and resurrection (mass incarceration), the peace of Christ (war), and the doctrines of creation and Incarnation/God's coming in Jesus's human flesh (climate change). These theological ideas will be explained in the individual chapters, but we reference them briefly here to indicate the central role that they will play in the arguments that we develop.

Why have a theological section at the center of each chapter? We live in a world where we believe ourselves condemned to support—or at the very least not to object too heavily to—death-dealing inequality, the caging and expulsion of people, the sacrifice of innocent civilians, and the destruction of the biosphere. These are facts of life that we may not like, but this seems to be the best we can hope for. We argue, by contrast, that Catholic belief and theology demand that alternatives be pursued. In order to be pursued, they must be imagined. Catholic theology provides some grounds for imagining something better than the life we currently lead. Each of these theological commitments represents an elaboration of Jesus's saying, "I came so that they might have life and have it more abundantly" (Jn 10:10). Our current condition of inequality, racism, and violence differs sharply from Jesus's vision of an abundant life. We write this book as theologians to invite you to contemplate a vision for the world, and for the way people live together, that aligns more closely with Christic abundant life.

The Politics of Mercy

This book's particular contribution to the Catholic social thought tradition and its imagining of a more abundant life relates to another Catholic tradition, the practice and theology of the **works of mercy**. To understand what these works are, we should first define **mercy**. This term can be defined by looking at the Latin word for it, **misericordia**, which incorporates *miseri*, which refers to suffering or pity, and *cor*, which means "heart." Thinking about these two roots, we can pose the following definition for mercy: it is the ability to feel another's suffering in one's own heart.

In a text composed for the World Meeting of Popular Movements in 2017, Francis writes that the primary threat or danger in the world is that we "disown our neighbors" and, by doing so, deny both their humanity and our own.[1] He uses the Good Samaritan parable (Lk 10:25–37) to shed light on this denial of humanity. By contrast, the parable defines what humanity is. Jesus's parable responds to a question from a lawyer, whom Jesus has been instructing in how to attain eternal life by loving God and neighbor. The lawyer asks, "Who is my neighbor?" (Lk 10:29). The parable, as paraphrased by Pope Francis, runs like this: a man who has been waylaid by robbers and left to die by the side of the road is ignored by two religious "elites" who, although they see the man in this dire strait, pass by on the road's other side. A Samaritan, a "foreigner, a pagan and unclean," does something different. He shows "true mercy" to the man: "he binds up the man's wounds, transports him to an inn, personally takes care of him, and provides for his upkeep." He draws near to the man, "to the point of identifying with him." Francis relates this parable to the current global economic system, which "has the god of money at its center." This system acts like the robbers. Global society often acts like the religious elites, looking "the other way with the pretence of innocence." Or at best we tend to look at the world's wounded through a screen, from a distance. In either case, global society "manifests an absence of true commitment to humanity." Jesus's parable teaches a different way to live. It answers not so much the question "who is my neighbor?" but "to whom should I be neighbor?" Francis appeals to his audience to struggle against a system that classifies others "in order to see who is a neighbor and who is not." Authentic humanity consists in having compassion in one's heart, "that capacity to suffer with someone else."

A year prior, during an Angelus blessing in St. Peter's Square, Francis ties together the Lukan parable of the Good Samaritan with the Matthean parable of the Sheep and the Goats (Mt 25:31–46).[2] He recommends that his listeners ask themselves, "Do I act as a neighbour or simply pass by? Am I one of those who selects people according to my own liking? It is good to ask ourselves these questions, and to ask them often, because in the end we will be judged on the works of mercy." Francis evokes the parable where Jesus the Judge announces his presence in the "least of these":

> The Lord will say to us: Do you remember that time on the road from
> Jerusalem to Jericho? That man who was half dead was me. Do you remem-
> ber? That hungry child was me. Do you remember? That immigrant who
> many wanted to drive away, that was me. That grandparent who was alone,
> abandoned in nursing homes, that was me. That sick man, alone in the
> hospital, who no one visited, that was me.

Francis cites specific examples of those our current world tends to
deem worthless, even less than human: the hungry child, the migrant,
the elders, and the sick. All of these people are equated with Christ.
Jesus himself is the man by the side of the road, abandoned by robbers
and ignored by many passersby. He identifies with those who need
mercy, the implication being that those who treat these people merci-
fully show mercy to Christ, fulfilling his law (see Gal 6:2).

The works of mercy, then, are acts of compassion for the suffering
of others. Traditionally these acts are divided into two types: the **corporal works of mercy**, which pertain to the needs of people's bodies
(Latin: *corpus*); and the **spiritual works of mercy**, which address the
needs of people's souls.

The corporal works of mercy have their genesis as a tradition in
Jesus's parable of the Last Judgment, which we just considered. They
are: feed the hungry, give drink to the thirsty, clothe the naked, ransom the captive, shelter the homeless, visit the sick, and bury the dead.
The spiritual works of mercy were consolidated as a tradition over the
course of the first four centuries of the church, as spiritual counterparts to the corporal works. They are: admonish the sinner, instruct
the ignorant, counsel the doubtful, comfort the afflicted, bear wrongs
patiently, forgive all injuries, and pray for the living and the dead. This
book's response to the crises of inequality, racism, and violence is
organized around the spiritual and corporal works of mercy.

Analogs to these elements are found in other traditions, but we
believe that the Catholic tradition brings them together in a uniquely
powerful way that can respond effectively to challenges in the present.
The approach we adopt in *The Politics of Mercy* is distinctive in at least
three ways:

- In contrast to secular models for addressing the crises we face,
  our approach is Catholic, and insists upon the importance of

a spiritual component in order to enliven our efforts and to strengthen our hope.

- In contrast to religious (and some secular) approaches that would argue for a charity alone approach, this book proposes a holistic culture of encounter and accompaniment that addresses crises locally and out of personal compassion, but also, when necessary, in wider society, through policies and laws, and through structural transformation, including economic structures. Such a holistic culture of encounter calls into question the binary that Brazilian Archbishop Helder Câmara criticized when he said, "When I give food to the poor, they call me a saint. When I ask why they are poor, they call me a communist."

- In contrast to secular approaches that reject charity and insist that justice alone can remedy the social challenges we face, this book insists on the centrality of charity and direct action to Catholic life. As Pope Benedict XVI avers in *Deus Caritas Est* (2005), the problem with approaches that focus on structural transformation and justice alone is that they sacrifice people in the present to a utopia of the future. This utopia is an imagined possibility that might never be realized. But the claim is that, in order to achieve this possibility, charitable work must end so that justice can take its place. Benedict contests this view:

> One does not make the world more human by refusing to act humanely here and now. We contribute to a better world only by personally doing good now, with full commitment and wherever we have the opportunity, independently of partisan strategies and programs. The Christian's program—the program of the Good Samaritan, the program of Jesus— is "a heart which sees." This heart sees where love is needed and acts accordingly. Obviously when charitable activity is carried out by the Church as a communitarian initiative, the spontaneity of individuals must be combined with planning, foresight and cooperation with other similar institutions. (*DC*, 31)

The politics of mercy is a multilevel application of the fourteen works of mercy, folding together spirituality, charity, and justice. We chose the word "politics" to describe this because "politics," if taken in the broadest sense of the Greek word *polis*, means a community of people, inclusive of both cities and rural areas. A **politics of mercy** is a way of gathering people together into community based in the ability to feel another's suffering in one's own heart. This kind of politics is being pursued by the Catholic organizations we describe in the conclusion to each chapter: Catholic Worker communities, Jesuit Refugee Service, Homeboy Industries, Catholic Relief Services, and Bethlehem Farm. We consider these examples to show that the politics of mercy is not just possible, but actual. Not only *can* it be lived; it *is* being lived. We must learn to live it and commit to living it more widely.

How to Use this Book

This book has three parts that correspond to the three realities mentioned in the book's subtitle: inequality, racism, and violence. Each part begins with a general introduction to these main topics. Within each part appear the book's five chapters: Chapter 1 on inequality (Part I), Chapter 2 on migration and Chapter 3 on mass incarceration (Part II), and Chapter 4 on war and Chapter 5 on climate change (Part III).

Each chapter is divided into five sections, namely:

- **Introduction:** stories about and/or data to describe a particular crisis.
- **Crisis:** consideration of the crisis, from both secular and theological points of view.
- **Catholic social thought:** texts from the Bible, encyclicals and other official documents, and theological ideas that can help us to formulate responses to the crisis.
- **Politics of mercy:** the politics of mercy at three levels: spiritual works of mercy, corporal works of mercy as charity, and spiritual and corporal works as a framework for structural transformation.
- **Conclusion:** presentation of exemplary Catholic communities that are living out the politics of mercy.

Each of the five chapters is organized around a basic contrast: a contemporary social crisis set against corresponding spiritual and corporal works of mercy. Inequality between wealth and poverty contrasts with the spiritual works of mercy of instructing the ignorant, counseling the doubtful, and comforting the afflicted, which are all works that help their practitioners train their attention so they may be vigilant and compassionate to neighbors in need. Inequality also contrasts (more obviously) with the corporal works of mercy of feeding the hungry, giving drink to the thirsty, and clothing the naked, which are works geared toward providing conditions for living with dignity. The migration crisis and mass incarceration, two crises related to racism, contrast with the spiritual works of mercy of admonishing the sinner, forgiving sinners, and bearing wrongs patiently, which foster in their practitioners virtues of reconciliation. The migration crisis contrasts with the corporal work of welcoming the stranger and mass incarceration with visiting the prisoner or, stated another way, ransoming the captive. War and climate change, both of which are crises of violence, contrast with the spiritual works of praying for the living and the dead and the corporal works of burying the dead and visiting the sick.

We should indicate just a few more features of the text. Within each chapter we have put in **boldface** key terms for understanding the chapter's topics. We have also provided references in endnotes, or in the case of official Church documents in parenthetical citations, though we have tried to keep these references to a minimum in order to avoid interrupting the flow of the text. Our bibliography shows the sources we consulted and cited here. We offer them as suggestions for further reading. We hope that these features of the book facilitate your learning and lead to vibrant conversations about Catholic life in our contemporary world.

As Catholics, we have hope for the future because we comprehend the resources available in our tradition to address the multifaceted crises that we face. We've accessed only some of them here, mindful that the tradition has a long history, covering numerous places, represented by a cloud of countless witnesses to our faith (see Heb 12:1). With this book we express the conviction that the Catholic tradition, though we all live it imperfectly, is always relevant, since it is rooted in Jesus Christ, whose merciful truth applies "yesterday, today, and forever" (Heb 13:8). In the scriptures, followers of Jesus are enjoined: "Always be ready to give an explanation to anyone who asks you for a reason for your hope" (1 Pet 3:15). We offer these chapters as reasons for our hope, asking that our readers consider weaving these reasons into their own.

Notes

1   Pope Francis, "Address of His Holiness Pope Francis to Participants in the Third World Meeting of Popular Movements," November 5, 2016, http://w2.vatican.va/content/francesco/en/speeches/2016/november/documents/papa-francesco_20161105_movimenti-popolari.html.

2   Pope Francis, "Angelus," July 10, 2016, https://w2.vatican.va/content/francesco/en/angelus/2016/documents/papa-francesco_angelus_20160710.html. The rest of the quotes in this paragraph are from this same address.

PART I

Inequality

RECENTLY, INEQUALITY HAS BEEN the central focus of the debate about a just economy. Much of what is said is shaped by a common-sense understanding of wealth that warrants reflection. Briefly stated, many people endorse an economic order based on private property rights and free markets. They note correctly that this economic order has created more wealth and brought more people out of poverty than any other system in world history. While proponents of the free market system acknowledge that it is not perfect, they contend that it is the most effective means of producing and distributing goods and providing for people's needs. As the world population grows and need grows along with it, they point out that our current system promotes vast economic growth. If extraordinary inequality is a byproduct of this growth, the argument continues, then so be it. People should benefit from their hard work, creativity, and capacity to create wealth. Why resent people who have succeeded? Why should we penalize people for creating wealth?

From a Catholic perspective, the economist Arthur Brooks has offered arguments that defend this understanding of the economic order.[1] His reasoning operates at multiple levels. First, he objects to critics who suggest that the free market system is problematic because it fails to distribute the wealth it generates in an equitable manner. Brooks describes this line of argumentation as the "**inequality trap**," by which he means that people demand perfection (complete equity) from a system that does not claim to be perfect (because this is, strictly speaking, impossible). He argues that the most effective rebuttal to this type of argument is to examine the existing economic options that are in fact available. He frames the options in a binary fashion: either death-dealing poverty or wealth inequality. While the norm for the majority of human beings in the history of civilization has been abject poverty, the free market system has performed an "economic miracle" by bringing billions of people out of poverty. Inequality may be a less-than-ideal byproduct of this system, but it is certainly preferable to early death due to lack of access to basic resources. Second, Brooks offers a moral-theological argument to justify this pragmatic line of argumentation. Catholic social teaching instructs us to care for the poor and to create political and economic structures that provide for a dignified life. Brooks maintains that no other system has been more successful at realizing these aims than the free market. From this perspective, Brooks argues that Catholics should affirm capitalism as an economic system that helps to build a more humane world. Furthermore, where some critics argue that capitalism promotes a culture of self-interest, competitive individualism, and indifference to the misfortunes of others, Brooks maintains that the economic system itself is neutral. Capitalism is neither "good" nor "bad." It is a system that can be used either to promote the common good or to exploit others for the benefit of the affluent. In this respect, Brooks argues that a Catholic approach to capitalism should affirm the moral potential of the free market system while recognizing the need to cultivate virtues among participants in order to ensure that it can be used to realize moral ends.

Pope Francis has offered an interpretation of inequality that contrasts with that of Brooks. Where Brooks sees capitalism as a system that generates a more inclusive order, Francis has diagnosed it as a system of exclusion that has generated a **throwaway culture.** A throwaway culture is a set of attitudes, customs, and institutions that presumes that "everything has a price, everything can be bought, everything is negotiable. This way of thinking has room only for a select few, while it discards all those who are unproductive."[2] In a throwaway culture, the market determines the value of things, and this value can change over time, depending on what is deemed fashionable or useful at a particular moment. Francis offers the concrete example of how a loss of 10 points in the stock market is deemed newsworthy, but neither the death of a homeless person from exposure to the cold nor children starving in various parts of the world generates any news coverage. These experiences are viewed as normal in a culture where certain people are viewed as disposable, and as a consequence "are thrown away like they are trash."[3]

Notably, Francis contests the way that Brooks has framed the challenge. Brooks basically assumes that inequality is normal. He judges it to be a necessary and perhaps even beneficial byproduct of a system that produces a great deal of wealth in the sense that it motivates competition. Francis is concerned that this type of worldview legitimates economic and cultural practices that fail to protect the basic dignity of every human person. A throwaway culture supports a broader **culture of indifference**, a set of attitudes, customs, and institutions that is impervious to or dismissive of suffering. Our contemporary culture of indifference prizes market values over human dignity. Market matters place first; mercy matters, second. Where Brooks wishes to relieve capitalism of any association with predatory greed or social indifference, Francis indicts the economic system for precisely this.

Pope Francis does not fully reject market economics. But he does offer substantial criticisms of contemporary free market economics from a moral and theological perspective. He encourages us to acknowledge honestly the real contradictions and failures of today's market economics and culture and the ongoing need for identifying alternatives. Pope John Paul II did this tremendously well in the encyclical *Centesimus Annus* (1991), when he examined the numerous failures of communism. This still remains to be done with regard to the dominant economic order of our day. Francis helps us to begin this process by rejecting the common-sense understanding that sees free market capitalism and state-run communism as the only two systems between which we must choose. Consequently, he feels no need to defend or to espouse either one. He sees the Catholic social thought tradition as offering ingredients for thinking about an economic alternative outside the extremes of capitalism and communism. In brief, they are:

- **Spiritual works of mercy:** These acts of care for the soul comprise a prayerful program for recognizing and protecting human dignity, in sharp contrast to a throwaway culture that assumes human worth to be tied to market measures. Spirituality is key, because it concerns what we are able to see and how we see it.

- **Corporal works of mercy:** As they have been interpreted by Catholic social thought, these acts of caring for people's bodily needs enact the Catholic commitment to integrating charity (as both a divine gift of love and as individual living out of that love) and justice (attempts to live out God's will at the level of social organization and political structures).

- **Universal destination of goods:** This moral principle recognizes the value of private property but sets it within the context of the doctrine of creation to clarify that the goods of creation should be distributed and shared in keeping with human dignity.

- **A social vision that properly balances economics, politics, and civil society:** A longstanding Catholic tradition holds that the three social spaces—the economy, the state, and civil society (family, voluntary organizations, etc.)—must work in concert, not letting one (for example, the market) dominate others.

We should note in closing that Francis's concern with inequality is not narrowly economic, not a matter of dollars and cents alone. It connects to the other crises we examine in subsequent chapters. In *Evangelii Gaudium* (2013), Francis observed: "inequality is the root of social ills" (*EG*, 202). Throughout his papacy, Francis has reflected on the connection between inequality and the ecological crisis, the rise of xenophobia, and political violence. Our decision to begin our discussion of the politics of mercy with inequality was quite intentional. It supports one of this book's central claims (which we borrow from Francis): "everything is connected." Inequality stands at the "root" of these other challenges, because inequality produces a cultural system that devalues certain people and intersects with other systems of exclusion and destruction that do the same: racism (devaluation of people with different skin pigmentation), war (devaluation of non-Americans), and environmental destruction (devaluation of non-human life). Thus the tone for a Catholic politics of mercy is set by the determination with which it aims to close the gap between wealth and poverty.

Notes

1   Arthur Brooks, "Confessions of a Catholic Convert to Capitalism," *America*, February 6, 2017, https://www.americamagazine.org/politics-society/2017/02/06/confessions-catholic-convert-capitalism.

2   Pope Francis, "Address of the Holy Father (Second World Meeting of Popular Movements, Bolivia)," July 9, 2015, http://w2.vatican.va/content/francesco/en/speeches/2015/july/documents/papa-francesco_20150709_bolivia-movimenti-popolari.html.

3   Pope Francis, "General Audience," June 5, 2013, http://w2.vatican.va/content/francesco/en/audiences/2013/documents/papa-francesco_20130605_udienza-generale.html.

CHAPTER 1

Wealth and Poverty

Introduction

HIGH ABOVE THE SLUMS of Mumbai rises a massive tower named Antilia. Its owner is the Indian steel magnate Mukesh Ambani, who as of November 2019 was the fifteenth-richest individual in the world and the richest person in Asia. Set amid slums where population density ranks among the highest in the world, the 27-story Antilia serves as a residence for Ambani's family—one family. And it is possible that they use the residence only occasionally. Arundhati Roy tells the story behind the name Antilia, suggesting why the Ambani family likely decided to label their home so strangely:

> Antilia is the name of a set of mythical islands whose story dates back to an 8th-century Iberian legend. When the Muslims conquered Hispania, six Christian Visigothic bishops and their parishioners boarded ships and fled. After days, or maybe weeks at sea, they arrived at the isles of Antilia where they decided to settle down and raise a new civilization. They burnt their boats to permanently sever their links to their barbarian-dominated homeland.[1]

It may be that the Ambanis hope to cut ties with the poverty of their homeland, raising a new civilization. "Antilia" is a perfect symbol of the attitude of a new global ruling class that has found novel ways of seceding from the rest of humanity. Journalist Jason Burke quotes the editor of an Indian design magazine as stating that Antilia indicates broader cultural trends: "We are heading into the sort of culture where money is not a question when setting up a home."[2] This may be true, but only for a tiny global minority.

For the "rest," the world offers fewer and fewer housing options, and for hundreds of millions globally, this means slums. Often, as with Antilia, these slums are located in direct proximity to the lavish residences of the wealthy. In Buenos Aires, the most expensive and famous part of town, Recoleta, home to the luxurious cemetery where generals, state leaders, and the rich and famous are buried, stands just across the tracks from the now almost-as-famous Villa 31, a notorious slum. As wealth rises in some sectors, slums agglomerate in others nearby.

Slums, a potent example of inequality, are largely located in the global South. The United Nations defines a slum as a place that combines several or all of the following five criteria: (1) inadequate access to safe water, (2) inadequate access to sanitation and infrastructure, (3) poor structural quality of housing, (4) overcrowding, and (5) insecure residential status.[3] Today, one-third of the world's urban population lives in slums. There exist more than 200,000 slums on earth, and around 1.3 billion people (14% of the global population) worldwide currently live in slums, a figure that could double by 2050 (30% of the global population).[4] These numbers, placed alongside inequality statistics—26 human beings possess as much total wealth as the bottom 50% of the global population (3.8 billion people)—serve as shocking reminders of the extreme inequality that defines our world.

In the United States, the same stark contrast exists. On Monday, August 5, 2019, a downturn in financial markets brought massive losses in wealth to the world's wealthiest people. The richest man in the world, Jeff Bezos, founder of Amazon.com, lost $3.4 billion in one day. He retained $110 billion in personal wealth to remain the world's wealthiest individual.[5] Two months earlier, Bezos went on an apartment shopping spree, spending $80 million on three condominiums.[6] This added to his personal stock of real estate, which in 2017 ranked as the 28th-largest in the United States, or roughly 20,000 acres.[7] By way of contrast, on any given night in the United States, over half a million people experience homelessness.[8] Roughly one-third of these people are families with children.

Homelessness serves as only one rather acute manifestation of poverty in the United States. While rarely talked about, 21% of children live in families below the federal poverty threshold. This means that a family of four is expected to live on $25,750 in 2019. Most estimates suggest that the average family of four would need twice that to live with some measure of stability and security, and over 43% of American families fail to meet this mark.[9]

While these data highlight the challenges that many families experience, the precarity of the average American often goes unnoticed. The data suggest that the majority of Americans live from paycheck to paycheck, with over 50% of the U.S. population reporting that they have less than $600 in a bank account.[10] Most Americans are one emergency away from total financial ruin. Many readers of this book—college students or parishioners in suburban parishes—very likely have a different experience of the economic health of the nation. But we should be aware that around half of our neighbors live in a situation of dire economic precarity.

The Crisis

Over the past two hundred years, the global economy has generated unprecedented levels of wealth. Recent decades have seen more people rise out of extreme poverty than ever before. These are undeniable and praiseworthy achievements of human ingenuity.

But the stories and the data that we have just explored demonstrate that all is not well. At the very least, it is worth asking whether and how we can accept the fact that some people can live in private skyscrapers while their neighbors live in slums, or why one man can afford to own 20,000 acres of land and multiple homes while half a million people cannot afford a single home. And it is worth pursuing the question of why so many children struggle to survive in a country known for its excess wealth.

The problem, it has long been recognized, is one of distribution. Recent studies have displayed the stark inequalities of wealth in our world. Thomas Piketty's 2013 book *Capital in the Twenty-First Century* stirred numerous conversations on this count. Piketty's argument is straightforward: the relatively stable social order produced after World War II in Europe and the United States is an aberration in the history of capitalism. Since 1975 we have reverted to the norm: that capitalism produces stark inequalities because the rate of growth of capital (profits, dividends, interest) outpaces the growth of labor wages (salaries and hourly pay). In a capitalist society, those with wealth see their fortunes grow more rapidly than middle-class wage laborers. The distance between the rich and poor grows ever more extreme. Piketty is a capitalist who affirms the real gains that have been created by the market. Still, he warns that a capitalist economy left unbalanced by a regulatory state that redistributes wealth will bring extreme political instability and will place society on a path toward disaster.

Piketty's concern about inequality in the economic realm has been affirmed and amplified by Pope Francis in his description of the contemporary economy. Most importantly for us, he reinterprets the issue theologically. Where Piketty's primary concern is with the destabilizing effects of inequality, Francis focuses on its systemic tendency to exclude poor and vulnerable populations. The theme of **social exclusion** is central for Francis. He links this secular theme to theological ideas of **sin**, particularly **structural sin** and **idolatry**.

Francis argues that today's world economy is an "economy of exclusion." Since economic matters are so central to people's lives, the result has been a widespread "culture of exclusion." According to Francis, while prior eras witnessed exploitation and oppression, which we still have, our era is distinctive for its tendency to exclude people, not only from the best things our economy provides, but even many basic goods. The world economy today leaves out vast populations. They are treated as "leftovers" (*EG*, 53). This word sums up Francis's diagnosis of what, from a Catholic point of view, we should pay attention to in the world economy. The main object of our attention should not be marvelous wealth, not even the marginal improvement from starvation to bare subsistence. Instead, it should be the people who are treated as disposable.

If we attend to this aspect of the world economy, Francis suggests, we can start to see the sins that set its foundation. Francis sees inequality as the chief manifestation of structural sin in our world. **Sin** is a breach of relationship with God and neighbor that stands contrary to God's will. It is usually seen as being perpetrated by individuals, through what they do or fail to do. Structural sin is a type of sin that transcends individual sin. **Structural sin** is a term from Catholic social thought that refers to social arrangements that violate love of neighbor and God's desire for justice, freedom, and peace. It comes about through individual sins, but grows beyond them, just as a skyscraper is built by the hands of individuals, but its presence goes far beyond what any one individual could accomplish.

We should read just a little bit of what Francis says about this in his own words. He writes: "The need to resolve the structural causes of poverty cannot be delayed … as long as the problems of the poor are not radically resolved by rejecting the absolute autonomy of markets and financial speculation and by attacking the structural causes of inequality, no solution will be found for the world's problems, or, for that matter, to any problems" (*EG*, 202). Addressing extreme inequality, which correlates with a culture of exclusion, is absolutely essential.

In addition to marking inequality as a prime example of structural sin, Francis has also spoken often about inequality in terms of **idolatry**. This word means the worship of false gods, or treating things that are not God as if they were God. Christianity, along with its parent tradition, Judaism, has at its center the proper worship of the one and only God. The first of the Ten Commandments states that God's people should "have no other gods before me" (Ex 20:3). The second commandment states that they should not make any idols (Ex 20:4–5). Soon after articulating these commandments, God adds that the people should not make gods of silver and gold (Ex 20:23). Throughout the writings of the Hebrew Scriptures, from the prophets and wisdom literature to the Psalms, and continuing into the New Testament, especially in the writings of Paul (e.g., 1 Cor 10:7), the Bible is unfailingly opposed to people taking anything to be a god that is not the one, living God. Throughout the centuries, Catholic tradition (admittedly sometimes in problematic ways, as with the murderous treatment of indigenous people for their religious practices) has opposed idolatry. Francis continues this tradition of insisting upon right worship of the one God by identifying an idolatrous impulse behind today's inequality and exclusion.

Shortly after he was elected pope, Francis offered the following description of the current cultural situation:

> Certain pathologies are increasing, with their psychological consequences; fear and desperation grip the hearts of many people, even in the so-called rich countries; the joy of life is diminishing; indecency and violence are on the rise; poverty is becoming more and more evident. People have to struggle to live and, frequently, to live in an undignified way. One cause of this situation, in my opinion, is in our relationship with money, and our acceptance of its power over ourselves and our society. Consequently the financial crisis which we are experiencing makes us forget that its ultimate

origin is to be found in a profound human crisis. In the denial of the pri-
macy of human beings! We have created new idols. The worship of the
golden calf of old (cf. Ex 32:15–34) has found a new and heartless image in
the cult of money and the dictatorship of an economy which is faceless and
lacking any truly humane goal."

What Francis engages in here is called **idolatry-critique**. He identifies
false worship for what it is: a cult that deviates from true religion, taking the impersonality of money as a god while turning away from the
personal God who loves each and every human person. He refers to the
"golden calf" episode in the Book of Exodus, during which God's chosen people, having grown impatient that they have not heard a message from God, fashion a "god" of their own out of gold, to which they
offer sacrifice. Even though they know that the god-calf is of their own
making, they worship it as a real god, expressing their devotion to it.
Something very similar, Francis implies, goes for today's global economy. People relate to money—a human creation—as having real power
over them. Thus people will commit, or at the very least be passively
involved in, all kinds of inhumanity in order to appease "the economy" or "markets."

Pope Francis's *Evangelii Gaudium* includes a section titled "no to
the new idolatry of money" (*EG*, 55–56). Francis suggests that today's
global economy drowns out the words of the gospel, inhibiting moral
and political life—and especially right worship of God. "Idolatry" is the
perfect descriptor. Idols shape cultures; they shape what we see and
fail to see. When the market is "deified" (*EG*, 56), the true and living
God becomes harder to notice. Wrong relationship or nonrelationship
with God generates a "culture of indifference" and a "culture of prosperity [that] deadens us" (*EG*, 53–54). Francis rejects, in no uncertain
terms, an economy characterized by extreme inequality:

> Just as the commandment "Thou shalt not kill" sets a clear limit in order
> to safeguard the value of human life, today we also have to say "thou shalt
> not" to an economy of exclusion and inequality. Such an economy kills....
> Can we continue to stand by when food is thrown away while people are
> starving? This is a case of inequality. Today everything comes under the
> laws of competition and the survival of the fittest, where the powerful feed
> upon the powerless. As a consequence, masses of people find themselves

excluded and marginalized: without work, without possibilities, without any means of escape. (*EG*, 53)

We have already acknowledged, and Francis does too, that today's global economy is incredibly adept at producing wealth. But Francis's idolatry critique also describes how effective the world economy is at putting people to death. Market trends fascinate us, leaving little time to notice, let alone care for, the homeless. To preserve food prices and markets as they are currently configured, massive amounts of food must be trashed, leaving people starving. Laws of competition guide us, making mercy seem an impossible dream. Consequently, people die: "men and women are sacrificed to the idols of profit and consumption."[12]

Catholic Social Thought

In the face of the theological diagnosis we have just explained, let's look to a set of Catholic teachings that could help communities to address the crisis of inequality. The first is **human dignity**. This is a comparatively new idea, at least in the way we talk about it today. It is rooted in an older one: the human person's creation as *imago Dei* (the image of God). We'll treat these two together. Then we'll discuss a related ethical principle that comes from Catholic social teaching: the **universal destination of goods**.

We'll begin by noting that all of these theological ideas originate with the doctrine of **creation**, the conviction that God made everything that is. Creation is attested throughout the Bible, most famously in the Book of Genesis (Gen 1–3), but also in many Psalms (Ps 8, 19, 29, 65, 104, 139, 148), the prophets (Is 48, 51), and the preaching of Jesus, which is filled with references to the wonders of God's creation (see, e.g., Mt 6:25–34, Lk 12:22–32). There are three basic corollaries to the doctrine of creation worth mentioning at the outset: all things are good (Gen 1:31), all things are God's (Ps 24:1; 1 Cor 10:26), and all things (for example, land) are lent to human persons, who must be guardians and protectors—but never outright owners—of them (see Lv 25:23). We'll discuss creation in more detail in Chapter 5, when we treat the crisis of climate change. For now we turn to material more directly related to the crisis of inequality.

The ongoing existence of extreme poverty around the globe and the continued deprivation experienced by millions of Americans threatens the very possibility of dignified life for a rapidly growing population. As such, it represents a grave violation of **human dignity**. Catholic tradition has insisted on the protection of human dignity because it is committed to the vision of the human person found in the Book of Genesis, the Psalms, and the prophets that human beings are created in the image and likeness of God, or ***imago Dei*** (Gen 1:26–27, 9:6; Ps 8:5; Is 64:8; 1 Cor 11:7). Because human beings are stamped with God's distinguishing mark, they have inestimably high worth. "Human dignity" signifies this worth, which is both a structure and a task inherent in every human person. According to Catholic teaching, by virtue of what the human person *is* and what she *does*, she has the possibility of aspiring, through Christ and the Holy Spirit's help, to share in God's own life, or the "divine nature" (2 Pet 1:4). Catholic tradition condemns encroachment on human dignity, especially (as happens too often today) among those who outwardly profess Christian faith while doing violence to their neighbors (see Jas 3:9).

In the twentieth century, the Catholic Church stated with greater explicit force than ever before that human persons have great dignity that must be respected in all cases. The major meeting of church leaders in the 1960s, the Second Vatican Council (Vatican II), dedicated one of its central documents, *Gaudium et Spes* (On the Church in the Modern World, 1965), to affirming and upholding human dignity as a central concern of twentieth-century Catholics. *Gaudium et Spes* maintains that each and every human person bears within her a "call to grandeur" (*GS*, 13) that comes from God. *Gaudium et Spes* insists that this call to grandeur must be answered in embodied ways; people are called to "glorify God in their bodies" (*GS*, 14). Grandeur and glorification seem to be, in the face of today's crisis of inequality, a tall order. Surely, as we have already acknowledged, the world economy's current configuration generates tremendous wealth and lifts people out of poverty. But often it lifts people into a level of bare survival (for example, from living on $1 per day to $2 per day), not to a level that facilitates their answering the call to grandeur. What we seek from a theological perspective is not mere survival, but a dignified life. Structures of exclusion, which preserve vast economic disparities, undermine a dignified life.

Benedict XVI provides particularly forceful reflections on human dignity in *Caritas in Veritate* (2009), where he contrasts human dignity and the demands of justice with widening wealth inequality (*CV*, 32). Later he insists, "On this earth there is room for everyone: here the entire human family must find the resources to live with dignity, through the help of nature itself—God's gift to his children—and through hard work and creativity" (*CV*, 50). Here Benedict brings the vision of *Gaudium et Spes* into the twenty-first century. In a world where slums proliferate for the many and skyscrapers rise for the few, it is important to declare that there is room for everyone. When the concentration of wealth makes it seem as if there is not room for everyone, that some people must be treated as scraps, Catholics must stand against this. We shall consider later in this chapter some proposals from Benedict and Francis regarding how human dignity might be better respected, but before then we must consider another theological idea: the ethical principle of the universal destination of goods.

The **universal destination of goods** is a principle that, like the idea of human dignity, has deep roots in ancient Catholic tradition but finds new articulation in more recent papal writings. The universal destination of goods is a multilayered concept, so let's view it in bullet points:

- Creation itself is an act of generosity and love by God.
- Since everything in creation results from love, all the goods of creation are meant to be used in such a way that they may be shared lovingly, that is, for the benefit of all.
- Such loving use by all entails mutual generosity (*charity*) and a social order that guarantees sacred rights of individuals (*justice*).

Having discussed these points, we should clarify the phrase itself. "Universal" means that all people should have enough of a share of the goods of creation to live out their human dignity. It means that we should accept responsibilities toward people in our immediate surrounding communities and our own nations, and not ask, "Am I my brother's keeper?" (Gen 4:9). But as "universal," our responsibilities to others extend beyond national boundaries. This is what is meant by "destination," which signifies where responsibilities are directed and where goods are going. And the word "goods" is used rather than simply "things," because we are talking about those *good* things that facilitate dignified living: nutritious food, clean water, adequate shelter, access to health care, and fruitful education.

The Catholic teaching on universal destination of goods theorizes the proper relationship between private property and the just use of creation. The principle of the universal destination of goods is rooted in the Bible and finds expression throughout the history of Christian theology (for example, in the preaching of early church saints such as Ambrose and John Chrysostom), but it has been revitalized in the twentieth and twenty-first centuries by Vatican II, Paul VI, John Paul II, and Francis. What has become a central claim of modern Catholic social thought—the proposition that the universal destination of goods should serve as the first principle of the social order—was first formulated by John Paul II in *Laborem Exercens* (1981) and has been repeated by Francis in *Laudato Si'* (2015). In *Laborem Exercens*, John Paul II notes that the church's tradition has never viewed the right to private property "as absolute and untouchable. Quite the contrary, it has always seen it in the broader framework of the common right of all to enjoy the goods of the creation; in other words, the right of private property is subordinate to the right of common usage, the destination of goods for all" (*LE*, 14). Put otherwise, the goods of creation were intended to provide dignified life for every human person. Our task is to ensure that all individuals have their basic needs met and have the capacity to live their call to grandeur and glorification.

It is worth noting that both the works of mercy and the universal destination of goods are filed in the *Catechism of the Catholic Church* under the seventh commandment: thou shall not steal (*CC*, 2447, 2402–06). If private property is not treated as a reality subordinate to the universal destination of goods, it is always in danger of degrading into theft.

To summarize the teaching on the universal destination of goods:

- The Catholic Church affirms the right to private property.
- It also affirms the right of the common usage of the goods of creation.
- It argues that common usage for the benefit of all precedes the right to private property.
- The implication of this is that the goods of creation should be redistributed either voluntarily (charity) or involuntarily (distributive justice) to ensure a dignified life for all human beings.

This fourth point begins to approach the issues that will be dealt with next, as we discuss a politics of mercy aimed at addressing the inequality between wealth and poverty.

The Politics of Mercy

How are Christians living out the theological ideas we have just learned? How may these theological ideas usher in a new society aimed at overcoming our current crisis of inequality? To answer these questions is to recognize and to envision a politics of mercy that incorporates spiritual work on ourselves (prayer and contemplation), charitable direct action, and the building of a new civilization of justice. The politics of mercy as it applies to our current crisis of inequality must center on three spiritual works of mercy: **instructing the ignorant**, **counseling the doubtful**, and **comforting the afflicted**, which we group together as works that train their practitioners in vigilance regarding others' needs. It combines these with three corporal works of mercy, which we group together as the works of mercy that provide for dignified life: **feeding the hungry**, **giving drink to the thirsty**, and **clothing the naked**. These apply most obviously to charitable direct action, but, particularly when they are paired with Francis's recent language of the "sacred rights" of lodging, labor, and land, they bring to light a civilizational program geared toward greater equality.

Spiritual Works of Mercy: Vigilance

Before we discuss charity and justice, we must consider how the politics of mercy flows out of a Christ-centered and Spirit-filled spirituality. Theological ethicist James Keenan, SJ, groups three of the traditional spiritual works of mercy—instructing the ignorant, counseling the doubtful, and comforting the afflicted—under the heading of works of mercy that train people in being vigilant.[13] They are spiritual practices that deepen one's relationship with God and, consequently, allow one to see the world more clearly. Though the spiritual works are directed from one person ("me") toward another, they often serve to change "me" first by nourishing the roots of my relationship with God. This deepening of relationship should redirect where people (both practitioners and recipients of these works) turn their eyes. We all need our attention redirected from time to time.

Keenan uses one of Jesus's parables to illustrate (Lk 16:19–31). Jesus tells the story of a rich man who lives with ample food, the finest drink, and the most luxurious clothing. Right outside his doorstep lies a poor man named Lazarus, whose destitution the rich man never notices. Both men die, and finally the rich man notices Lazarus, but only because Lazarus has ended up in heaven and the rich man in Hades. The rich man attempts to order Lazarus around, requesting a drink. Jesus relates this parable to depict what it looks like *not* to live out God's commands. One could say that the rich man's primary sin is against vigilance. He fails to see his neighbor in need. The implication of Jesus's parable is that wealth is precisely what makes the rich man blind to Lazarus's suffering. In a world marked by the crisis of inequality, many of us fail to see Lazarus at our doorstep. So many of us—rich and poor—point our admiring gazes toward the healthy and the wealthy. A misturned gaze has real-world effects that become especially dire when we recognize that the gaze misturned toward wealth has structured our economies, governments, societies, neighborhoods, and daily lives.

Christians must recognize that Jesus calls them to be shaped by the **theological virtues**: divine gifts of **faith, hope, and charity**, which train people in vigilance, vision, and sympathy. The **spiritual works of instruction, counsel, and comfort** facilitate such shaping.

The spiritual work of instructing the ignorant draws its strength from the gift of faith. To see how, we have to understand **faith** properly. It's not simply belief. It is loyalty—fidelity, or *being* faithful. In the Christian, theological sense, it is loyalty to the God of Jesus Christ, empowered by the Holy Spirit. Ignorance is not simply lack of knowledge. Instead, ignorance refers to what we ignore or attend to based on where our loyalties or fidelities lie. The person living out this spiritual work must self-examine first, in order to discover whether her faith is properly directed by God toward God. We've already discussed how wealth functions as an idol; this idolatry brings distorted faith and ignorance. A politics of mercy that addresses inequality would begin with the spiritual work of fostering in oneself and others God-directed faith and proper vigilance to today's Lazaruses.

Something similar would go for the spiritual work of counseling the doubtful. The divine gift of **hope** sustains it. Hope is not bare expectation. It is joyful waiting for new life. In the Christian, theological sense, it is waiting in joyful anticipation, with the Spirit's help, for God's will to be done on earth as it is in heaven (Mt 6:10). The person living out this spiritual work should take stock of her hopes and see whether they outshine or are overshadowed by her doubts. The case often made for why inequality is not quite a crisis stems from doubt that an alternative to our current global economic order does or can exist. A politics of mercy that addresses inequality would continue by strengthening the vision of alternatives to the system that casts off Lazaruses, alternatives that would align with God's will that human persons recognize, rather than doubt, their shared dignity.

Charity propels the spiritual work of comforting the afflicted. The First Letter of John states plainly that God is love (1 Jn 4:16). The Greek word for "love" in this case is *agâpe*, which is translated into Latin as *caritas*, or charity. This love is the kind that the world tends not to give: a deep, self-giving, and merciful love that comes as a gift from God. In a culture where we offer our devotion to health and wealth, to love a person who is suffering and downtrodden—or to feel loved when we are suffering or downtrodden—is a miracle. It defies expectations. The spiritual work of comforting the afflicted stems from a person's self-examination, where he confronts himself with the question of what he loves most. A prime goal of Christian life is, eventually, to be able to answer this question by saying, "I love those whom God loves most, those Lazaruses among us whom people usually count as the least." A spirituality based on the works of mercy, which can guide actions of charity and justice, turns the values of this world on their head. Were such a spirituality put into practice in our era of extreme inequality, market matters would give way to mercy matters. And it just so happens that some Catholic organizations are doing this.

Charity: Food, Drink, Clothing

Numerous Catholic organizations work every day to feed people and to give them drink, to clothe them, and to defend their rights to basic necessities of everyday life. Catholic Charities USA, for example, has labored for over a century to ensure poor people's access to proper nutrition by operating and partnering with food banks, food pantries, and community farms.[14] In this book, we characterize such efforts as forms of direct, charitable action. This is a key component of a Catholic politics of mercy. The Catholic tradition endorses a number of different types of responses to social crises, but it places central emphasis on charity put into practice as direct action. Such practice is also called **almsgiving**, or free giving of money, goods, time, effort, and/or attention to the poor.

The centrality of charity to Catholic life from a biblical perspective is perhaps best summarized by Jesus's injunction in his parable on the Last Judgment to feed the hungry, give drink to the thirsty, and clothe the naked (Mt 25:31–46). In *Charity: The Place of the Poor in the Biblical Tradition*, Gary Anderson observes that this parable is a central text in the development of the early church's reflection on the importance of charity to Catholic life. One reason that early Christians came to view charity as critical to Catholic life is that they took this parable literally. It teaches that we encounter Christ himself through the charitable acts that we do "for the least of these." Charity is a **sacramental** act, a sign through which one encounters God. Catholics should continually keep in mind this theological and sacramental dimension of working with the poor and marginalized to facilitate their dignified living.[15]

In addition to its scriptural roots and sacramental character, charity is linked to Catholic teaching on **subsidiarity**. This concept is first formulated by Pius XI in *Quadragesimo Anno* (1931). The concept holds that social needs and problems should be addressed at the most local level possible. In response to homelessness in a city, from a Catholic perspective the first step should not be to appeal to the federal government, but to mobilize local resources to attempt to respond to the problem.

The rationale behind this focus on local action is twofold. First, Catholic tradition prioritizes direct action because of its **personalism**: individual persons are of inestimably high value, and all individual persons should take responsibility for upholding and defending each other's dignity at a personal level. Large governmental organizations should not be appealed to first to rectify social issues, since this could rob individuals and communities of the opportunity to encounter God in the poor. Second, and more pragmatically, the Catholic tradition maintains that people on the ground in local communities will have a better understanding of the culture and the needs of that community than remote government officials. For instance, a member of the local community might know about the specific causes of homelessness in her area, and likely would also be familiar with the organizations that could provide aid, assistance, and care for those experiencing homelessness.

It is important to understand that the principle of subsidiarity does not exclude intervention from federal governments or international organizations. When local organizations and governments lack the power or resources to respond to people's needs, national and international responses are warranted. We will see shortly that Pope Benedict XVI calls for the creation of an international body that regulates the global economy and redistributes resources in response to the global challenge of poverty. Benedict affirms the ongoing need for charitable forms of direct action. He also recognizes that in an era of globalized economy, it is impossible to respond effectively to poverty and inequality at the local level alone.

Justice: Sacred Rights

The theological tradition of the *imago Dei* and respecting human dignity points us toward a political rendering of the corporal works of mercy that provides not just for the basic necessities of life of food, drink, and clothing, but also, as Francis argues, for a broader set of **sacred rights** that include **land, lodging**, and **labor**. Such expanded provision would facilitate dignified living and not just mere survival. Many proponents of the current system celebrate that survival has been provided. But survival should be *assumed*, not cheered. What should be celebrated is a world in which dignified, abundant life is the universal norm. A politics of mercy conforming to the spiritual works of instruction, counsel, and comfort and the corporal works of feeding, giving drink, and clothing, would require us to think and act anew with respect to inequality in our world. In the introduction, we noted that Catholic social teaching emphasizes the importance of both charity and justice in its approach to social problems. Where charity responds immediately to social misfortune and attempts to mitigate it through direct acts of service, a commitment to social justice seeks to develop laws, rights, social structures, and cultures that ensure that the basic dignity of each individual is protected.

In Bolivia in 2015, Francis called for the creation of economic and political structures that guarantee the three "Ls" ("Ts" in Spanish) of land, labor, lodging (*tierra, trabajo, techo*) to all human beings. In a speech given the same year in the Kangemi slums in Nairobi, Kenya, Francis elaborated this vision for social rights by insisting "that every family has dignified housing, access to drinking water, a toilet, reliable sources of energy for lighting, cooking and improving their homes ... that basic services are provided to each of you; that your appeals and your pleas for greater opportunity can be heard; that all can enjoy the peace and security which they rightfully deserve on the basis of their infinite human dignity."[16] For Francis, the excluded people of the world should have their basic needs met as rights, and this should be the baseline focus for daily struggle. He approves of the quotidian actions of popular movements that aim to provide the three Ls, and with them, food for the hungry, drink for the thirsty, and clothing for the naked. He reminds Christians that their charge to distribute the fruits of the land and of work is stronger than philanthropy and moral obligation; "it is a commandment." Constructively, Francis advocates for a "truly communitarian economy" in which "the economy should not be a mechanism for accumulating goods, but rather the proper administration of our common home. This entails a commitment to care for that home and to the fitting distribution of its goods among all." Rather than wealth concentration, which is the prevailing model's dominant imperative, protection of the sacred rights of the poor must become our economic target.

The call for land and lodging for everyone may sound radical. But it follows directly from Catholic social teaching on the universal destination of goods. Francis's demand that these rights be protected subverts the commonly held view in American culture that people should be guaranteed the "opportunity" to purchase some land or a home and to compete for work in the labor market. Francis's demand is thoroughly consistent with the Catholic affirmation of the right to private property, with the qualification that property should be distributed as broadly as possible to ensure that it benefits everyone, not only the wealthy. If the current economic system prevents segments of the population from access to land, lodging, and even labor, then the system is inadequate from a Catholic perspective.

Benedict XVI's social vision is helpful in thinking more concretely about how to build a social order in which people's sacred rights are respected and protected. In particular, the Catholic vision for the social order that he presents in *Caritas in Veritate* (2009) offers a particularly compelling **communitarian** vision of society wherein the three distinct spaces of **economy, state**, and **civil society** work in harmony to produce a social order that protects the dignity of each individual. As the title of the encyclical suggests, charity stands at the center of Benedict's vision, which he views as a reality that is neither external to economics and politics, nor purely privatized and individualized. Out of this principle, Benedict offers his account of the relationship between the three major social spaces.

According to Benedict, each space is governed by its own logic: the economy (commercial logic), the state (the logic of justice), and civil society (the logic of the gift). Benedict describes the economy as a legitimate, distinct social space with its own logic: commercial logic (*CV*, 36). When properly ordered, it is a social institution that supports the exchange of goods and services that allows basic societal needs to be met (*CV*, 35). This social institution's logic is properly ordered when it observes **commutative justice**, or fair exchange, between consenting parties. While the economy and markets have their own legitimacy, running the economy on commercial logic alone leads to distorted social relations and "grave imbalances" in society (*CV*, 36). The economy operating strictly on its own devices cannot perform even its own tasks: "Without internal forms of solidarity and mutual trust, the market cannot completely fulfil its proper economic function" (*CV*, 35). Solidarity and mutuality come from the other two social spaces.

In the realm of civil society, Benedict argues that the governing logic is that of the gift, which he describes as moral impulse that leads individuals to act on the basis of a commitment to the common good rather than individual self-interest. The **logic of the gift** represents an integral dimension of economic activity, not as a supplement but rather as an internal, guiding norm (*CV*, 36).

The same goes for the political order. It plays a critical role in developing a just social order. To the economic space's model of justice, commutative justice, the political adds **distributive justice** (*CV*, 36, 39), by which the wealth created in society is redistributed so that each person's basic dignity is protected and provided for. Benedict even goes so far as to call for a global political authority with the power to regulate the economy and to ensure food security and basic economic rights for the global population (*CV*, 67). Although this suggestion has been dismissed as impractical, this is precisely the type of creative thinking necessary to confront inequality. And it fits exactly with a proper understanding of the principle of subsidiarity: given the global extent and severity of wealth inequality, a global political solution has become inevitable.

The proper interrelation among these three social spaces is necessary to build a just and equitable social order. The economic space must be shaped by moral impulses (the logic of the gift) and regulated by distributive justice (the logic of justice), but even more remarkably, these commitments need to be internalized within economic activity, because "every economic decision has a moral consequence," and it is necessary for justice to be applied "*to every phase of economic activity*" (*CV*, 37).

Because economic activity is now globalized and no longer circumscribed by the boundaries of nation-states, it is difficult for governments to perform their distributive function. It is no longer tenable to assume that the wealth generated in the private sector can be effectively redistributed by national political authorities alone. As a consequence, "the canons of justice must be respected from the outset, as the economic process unfolds, and not just afterwards or incidentally" (*CV*, 37). The only way to ensure this is to reimagine economics from the inside out, with the logics of gift and distributive justice reconfiguring commercial logic from within. This demands the creation of new forms of economic activity that freely choose to pursue ends other than "pure profit" (*CV*, 37).

At its core, *Caritas in Veritate* calls for the reorganization of market economics on a new foundation, a level that is deeper than this world: God's love and truth revealed in Christ. This foundation would support commercial activity—not denigrating business, not ridding the world of private property, not abolishing markets, or anything else like this. But the foundation rules out preeminence or dominance of the market over other spaces. Importantly, this is Francis's primary concern—namely, that the market now rules political and social life. The market, as an idol, distorts both political and social life and robs society of the resources necessary to build a more equitable and just world. Benedict does not endorse any concrete economic-political paradigm as an alternative to the current economy. But his emphasis on the importance of "economic democracy" (*CV*, 38) and his call for an international body to oversee capitalism signals a significant break with capitalism as we know it. In this respect, Benedict's comment that "in many respects, democratic socialism was and is close to Catholic social doctrine and has in any case made a remarkable contribution to the formation of a social consciousness" points to the distance between his social vision and that of proponents of American-style "democratic capitalism" like Arthur Brooks.[17]

In a world that witnessed the largest increase in billionaires in history in 2017 (the world now has 2,043 billionaires), and in which 26 people possess as much wealth as the bottom 50% of the global population (3.8 billion people), can the protection of the sacred rights of the poor (Francis) mean anything other than the massive redistribution of wealth in the realm of civil society (charity) and political life (justice)?[18] Whether we term this a society built upon the foundation of the logic of the gift (Benedict XVI) or a culture of mercy (Francis), what is evident is that real and substantive change is not only *possible*, but *necessary*. This need for an alternative to the current system is a clear implication of the priority of the universal destination of goods in Catholic social teaching.

Let us conclude this section by taking note of how Francis describes the duty of justice in this context:

> ...we can no longer sustain unacceptable economic inequality, which prevents us from applying the principle of the universal destination of the earth's goods. We are all called to undertake processes of apportionment which are respectful, responsible and inspired by the precepts of distributive justice.... One group of individuals cannot control half of the world's resources. We cannot allow for persons and entire peoples to have a right only to gather the remaining crumbs. Nor can we be indifferent or think ourselves dispensed from the moral imperatives which flow from a joint responsibility to care for the planet, a shared responsibility often stressed by the political international community, as also by the Magisterium.[19]

Justice—both distributive and commutative—requires more equitable sharing of the goods of God's creation. This equity is a prime goal of a Catholic politics of mercy.

Conclusion: The Catholic Worker

Because Catholic life is universal—the Greek word *katholikos* translates as "universal"—the tradition affirms diverse ways of responding
to Christ's call to care for the poor that are appropriate for individuals
and communities. The work of Dorothy Day and the Catholic Worker
movement serves as a radical example in twentieth-century America
of the attempt to respond to Christ's injunction in Matthew 25 to feed
the hungry, give drink to the thirsty, and clothe the naked. That witness demands continually renewed attention in the twenty-first century, our current era of inequality.

Dorothy Day (1897–1980) converted to Catholicism in 1927 after
a vibrant young life as a socialist and radical journalist. In 1933, with
Peter Maurin (1877–1949), she founded the Catholic Worker movement, which sought to create intentional communities (houses of hospitality and agrarian farms) that aimed to transform the social order by
performing the spiritual and corporal works of mercy.

The work of the Catholic Worker movement is rooted in a Catholic
personalism that views each person as the occasion to encounter
God. This conviction serves as the basis for the movement's distinctive approach to social transformation, in which the task is not simply
to alleviate social problems, but to do so in a way that is befitting of
inviolable dignity of the people involved. The Catholic Worker movement prioritizes forms of direct action that enable those who work at
houses of hospitality to spend time with the people they serve, to learn
their names and their stories, and to treat each and every person they
encounter as Christ in their midst. This personalist approach to charitable action represents a central feature of Catholic Worker spirituality, but on its own it represents only a partial response and should be
supplemented with a vision for transforming the entire social order.
For instance, Day observed, "To feed the hungry, clothe the naked
and shelter the harborless without trying to change the social order
so that people can feed, clothe, and shelter themselves, is just to apply
palliatives."[20] The spiritual and corporal works of mercy serve simultaneously to respond to others' concrete suffering *and* to build transformative forms of community.

Day called for a "permanent revolution" that sought social transformation not through the power of the state or a competitive economy, but rather through individuals voluntarily deciding to practice

the spiritual and corporal works of mercy in their daily lives. Day explains: "We consider the spiritual and corporal Works of Mercy and the following of Christ to be the best revolutionary technique and a means for changing the social order rather than perpetuating it."[21] Is it really possible that a renewed commitment to the spiritual and corporal works of mercy can support the type of "revolution" that Day views as central to Catholic social teaching? Here as elsewhere she follows Christ's example. Robert Coles notes that Day was committed to the use of "Christ's technique" as a response to social problems: "She was always trying to remember that He was an obscure carpenter who, in His early thirties, did not go talk with emperors and kings and important officials, but with equally obscure people."[22] Because Day modeled her approach to social change on the life of Jesus Christ, she thought the standard approach to politics should be reconceived. Her personalist form of politics served as an alternative to large-scale political operations that attempted to transform the social order from centers of economic and political power. Day was well aware that this alternative would be viewed as a failure by the standards of the world. The charitable work that the Catholic Worker movement does in houses of hospitality is very small by the world's standards, but "it is like the little boy with a few loaves and fishes. Christ took that little and increased it. He will do the rest. What we do is so little we may seem to be constantly failing. But so did he fail. He met with apparent failure on the Cross. But unless the seed fall into the earth and die, there is no harvest. And why must we see results? Our work is to sow."[23] The task is not to ensure immediate and tangible success, but rather to place one's faith in God and to go about the work of doing what Christ instructed his disciples to do by feeding the poor, giving drink to the thirsty, and clothing the naked.

Day's legacy in American Catholicism is immense, both in terms of the continued work of Catholic Worker houses of hospitality and of her retrieval of a biblical spirituality rooted in a literal adherence to the Sermon on the Mount and the parable of Last Judgment in Matthew 25. To this day the Catholic Worker runs houses of hospitality that serve the poor and homeless. There are currently houses of hospitality in over 150 cities in the United States. Houses of hospitality provide food, drink, and shelter to thousands of poor and homeless each and every day of the year. These houses are run by volunteers who live in an intentional community that integrates the spiritual and corporal works of mercy in the rhythm of their daily lives.

The Catholic Worker movement's approach, which so heavily emphasizes direct action, may in fact require political supplementation. It could be brought into productive conversation with Benedict's social vision and Francis's call for societal protection of the three sacred rights. Such a conversation would help to ensure that Catholics respond to global inequality with a proper *politics* of mercy. But even without this political supplement, the Catholic Worker movement serves as perhaps the most compelling example of what it looks like to live out a commitment to upholding human dignity, to avoiding fascination with the idol of wealth, and to practicing vigilance for the Lazaruses in our midst. In the wake of the 2008 financial crisis, Jim Consedine of the Catholic Worker in Christchurch, New Zealand, wrote: "Just imagine if the one billion Catholics all took a stand for economic justice in their lives and in society. It's a pipe dream—but the world would change overnight, and economic justice would be seen in every street."[24]

Notes

1   Arundhati Roy, *Capitalism: A Ghost Story* (New York: Haymarket Books, 2014), 46.

2   Jason Burke, "Mukesh Ambani, India's Richest Man, Builds World's First Billion-Dollar Home," *The Guardian*, October 13, 2010, https://www.theguardian.com/world/2010/oct/13/mukesh-ambani-india-home-mumbai.

3   See the website for the United Nations Programme for Human Development (UN-Habitat), "Slum Upgrading," https://unhabitat.org/topic/slum-upgrading.

4   This estimate, which has been widely cited, comes from a 2003 report from UN-Habitat, the United Nations settlement program. See UN-Habitat, *The Challenge of Slums: Global Report on Human Settlements 2003* (London: Earthscan Publications, 2003), xxv.

5   Devon Pendelton, "World's Richest Lose 117 Billion," August 5, 2019, https://www.bloomberg.com/news/articles/2019-08-05/world-s-richest-lose-117-billion-in-one-day-market-meltdown.

6   Caroline Cakebread and Katie Warren, "Jeff Bezos Is Dropping $80 Million," *Business Insider*, June 4, 2019, https://www.businessinsider.com/ jeff-bezos-owns-five-massive-homes-across-the-united-states-2017-10.

7   "The Land Report 100," *The Land Report*, https://www.landreport.com/ americas-100-largest-landowners/.

8   U.S. Department of Housing and Urban Development, "The 2018 Annual Homeless Assessment Report," December 2018, https://files.hudexchange .info/resources/documents/2018-AHAR-Part-1.pdf.

9   National Center for Children, "Child Poverty," http://www.nccp.org/topics/ childpoverty.html.

10 Adrian Garcia, "Most Americans Wouldn't Cover a 1K Emergency with Savings," *Bankrate*, January 16, 2019, https://www.bankrate.com/banking/savings/ financial-security-january-2019/.

11 Pope Francis, "Address of Pope Francis to the New Non-Resident Ambassadors to the Holy See: Kyrgyzstan, Antigua, and Barbuda, Luxembourg, and Botswana," May 16, 2013, http://w2.vatican.va/content/francesco/en/speeches/2013/may/ documents/papa-francesco_20130516_nuovi-ambasciatori.html.

12 Francis, "General Audience," June 5, 2013, http://www.vatican.va/con-tent/francesco/en/audiences/2013/documents/papa-francesco_20130605_ udienza-generale.html. As with Benedict's criticism of Marxism as a sacrificial ideology, Francis describes capitalism as a form of idolatry that "sacrifice(s) human lives on the altar of money and profit." In both cases, it is a theolog-ical error that generates an ethos of sacrifice. Pope Francis, "Address of the Holy Father (Paraguay)," July 11, 2015, http://w2.vatican.va/content/francesco/ en/speeches/2015/july/documents/papa-francesco_20150711_paraguay-societa-civile.html.

13 James F. Keenan, SJ, *The Works of Mercy: The Heart of Catholicism,* 3rd ed. (Lanham, MD: Rowman & Littlefield, 2017), 81–86. For the next several paragraphs, we are extending Keenan's insights to develop our description of a Catholic politics of mercy.

14 For more information on this work of Catholic Charities USA, see https://www .catholiccharitiesusa.org/our-ministry/food-nutrition/.

15 Gary Anderson, *Charity: The Place of the Poor in the Biblical Tradition* (New Haven, CT: Yale University Press, 2013), 6.

16 Pope Francis, "Address of the Holy Father (Kangemi Slum in Nairobi, Kenya)," November 27, 2015. http://w2.vatican.va/content/francesco/en/speeches/2015/november/documents/papa-francesco_20151127_kenya-kangemi.html.

17 Benedict XVI, *Values in a Time of Upheaval* (San Francisco: Ignatius Press, 2006), 144.

18 Diego Alejo Vázquez Pimentel, Iñigo Macías Aymar, and Max Lawson, "Reward Work, Not Wealth," Oxfam International, January 22, 2018, https://www-cdn.oxfam.org/s3fs-public/file_attachments/bp-reward-work-not-wealth-220118-summ-en.pdf; Oxfam International, "Five Shocking Facts about Extreme Global Inequality," https://www.oxfam.org/en/5-shocking-facts-about-extreme-global-inequality-and-how-even-it.

19 Pope Francis, "Address to Participants in the International Forum on 'Migration and Peace,'" February 21, 2017. http://w2.vatican.va/content/francesco/en/speeches/2017/february/documents/papa-francesco_20170221_forum-migrazioni-pace.html.

20 Dorothy Day, "More about Holy Poverty, Which Is Voluntary Poverty," *The Catholic Worker* (February 1945), 1–2.

21 Dorothy Day, *The Long Loneliness* (New York: Harper & Row, 1952; repr. 1997), 186.

22 Robert Coles, *Dorothy Day: A Radical Devotion* (Reading, MA: Perseus, 1987), 90. For Day's reflections on this point, see Day, *The Long Loneliness*, 204–5.

23 Dorothy Day, *Selected Writings* (Maryknoll, NY: Orbis Books, 2005), 92.

24 Jim Consedine, "Faith and the Financial Crisis," *Houston Catholic Worker* 29, no. 1 (January–February 2009), https://cjd.org/2009/02/01/faith-and-the-financial-crisis/.

PART II

Racism

WHAT IS RACISM? WE need to clarify what this reality is, because it will form the primary background for these two chapters. Further, because there are so many understandings of this reality that circulate in the public, we should be as precise as possible about what it does and does not mean. We must also be clear about the multiple forms it takes. Racism is not singular. It is not monolithic. The objective of this introduction is to lay out some of the complexities of the topic.

To start, we can define **racism** as the meaning attached to differences in skin pigmentation. Importantly, these differences are assigned a social status, so that whiteness confers social advantage and color confers social disadvantage. The common-sense understanding of racism often points to direct acts of bigotry such as personal prejudice, demeaning language, and intentional acts of exclusion (for instance, expressing bias toward groups other than one's own, using well-known slurs, or barring persons of certain racial or ethnic groups from sitting with others at a lunch counter). This definition of racism allows people to claim that they have no part in racism, because they view it as an individual and intentional attitude or activity. Certainly, racism does involve these types of things, but we must understand that it is far more than this. We would characterize what we've been discussing as **direct racism**, but this is only one form among others.

There are at least four forms of racism: **direct**, **unconscious**, **strategic**, and **structural**. Each of them operates in a different way (explicitly or implicitly) and at a different level (individual or collective). Let us explain what these forms are and how they function, offering a few examples of each.

- **Direct racism:** intentional speech and acts disparaging a person or group on the basis of skin pigmentation.
  - Racial epithets
  - Segregation
- **Unconscious racism:** a form of racism that is not conscious or deliberate, but which relies on cultural tropes that function to shape our perception of others to stoke fear and contempt.
  - Association of "blackness" with "criminality"
  - Association of "brownness" with "illegality"
  - Association of "Arab" with "terrorist"
- **Strategic racism:** a form of political or cultural speech that attempts indirectly to communicate contempt for or disregard of particular social groups in order to garner social or political advantage.
  - "Dog whistle" racism—for example, politicians' use of coded phrases such as "welfare queens," "super predators," or "chain migration"
- **Structural racism:** ways in which racism is codified into law and custom in order to persecute, exclude, and disadvantage particular groups.
  - Jim Crow, redlining, mass incarceration, Chinese Exclusion Act (1882)

These four forms all intersect with one another, and as they interact they amplify each other. We can think about it in terms of a diagram in which each circle stands for a distinct form of racism, and the many arrows (there could probably be more!) that cut across the different circles indicate interactions and influences between the types of racism.

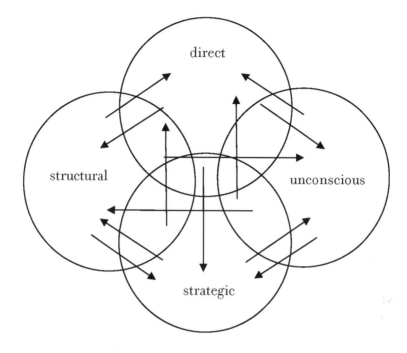

Figure II.1: Interactions and influences among four forms of racism.

The best way to explain this diagram is to illustrate with an example. Let's consider the Jim Crow–era South in the United States, where the four forms of racism were exhibited as follows:

- **Direct:** marking people as "colored" or the n-word; lynching and violent attacks
- **Unconscious:** fear that black men will "violate" white women
- **Strategic:** Southern Democratic politicians running on a platform of preserving white privilege; using "dog whistles" and overt racism to mobilize whites to support candidates and policies
- **Structural:** segregation codified as law: schools, buses, restaurants

One could start at any point among these four and see how racism circulates through these distinctive forms. If we start at the level of unconscious racism, for example, the unconscious tendency to view black people as inferior to whites or inherently sexualized or violent can authorize direct attacks (verbal or physical violence), the institution of laws and customs that ensure inferior social status and control (segregation), and political strategies aimed at winning elections by voicing racist thoughts and supporting racist public policies (Dixiecrats).

The point is that each form of racism contributes to, amplifies, replicates, and alters other forms of racism. There are various ways of naming this constellation of four forms of racism. We have already used the language of social advantage and disadvantage. One could also speak of the social hierarchy instituted based on assumptions about skin pigmentation. Others call it **white supremacy**. This term has the benefit of specifically naming the type of skin pigmentation to which benefits accrue and which lands at the top of the hierarchy. Although this term tends to be associated with groups like the KKK, neo-fascism, and white nationalism, it has a broader meaning that signifies the fact that white people sit at the top of the racial hierarchy and—whether through direct, unconscious, strategic, or structural means—accrue the benefits.

With regard to Catholic social thought, Bryan Massingale observes in *Racial Justice and the Catholic Church* that the most important thing to note about it on the issue of racism in society is that there is very little of it.[1] Outside of Pope Pius XI's 1937 document *Mit Brennender Sorge: On the Church and the German Reich*, which denounced the racism of Nazi anti-Semitism, and the U.S. Catholic Bishops' statement on *Discrimination and Christian Conscience* (1958), there is no official statement on racism in the Catholic tradition prior to Vatican II. Even at Vatican II, the only document to explicitly raise the issue was *Gaudium et Spes*, which mentioned race only a handful of times in the context of discussions of broader social divisions in the world. After Vatican II, the Pontifical Council for Justice and Peace produced two important analyses of racism: *The Church and Racism: Toward a More Fraternal Society* (1988) and *Contribution to World Conference Against Racism: Racial Discrimination, Xenophobia, and Related Intolerance* (2001).

In 2018, the United States Conference of Catholic Bishops published its most comprehensive treatment of racism to date, *Open Wide Our Hearts: The Enduring Call to Love*. It describes the struggle against racism as a "life" issue (*OW*, 30) and acknowledges the Catholic Church's complicity in America's racist history through its participation in the colonization of indigenous populations and the trans-Atlantic slave trade (*OW*, 21–22). Additionally, the document offers a more sophisticated analysis of the different forms of racism than did previous documents by narrating the histories of oppression and exclusion that have shaped the lives of generations of African American, Latinx, and Native American communities (*OW*, 10–14).

But even as *Open Wide Our Hearts* represents a significant improvement over previous church documents, it still does not go as far as one would hope in its response to twenty-first-century racism. In the document, the bishops describe racism as the conscious and unconscious act of holding one's "own race or ethnicity as superior" and other races and ethnicities as "inferior and unworthy of equal regard" (3). And while the document does periodically recognize that racism exists within structures and institutions, the focus remains on racism as an interpersonal transgression that demands a personal response ("open wide our hearts"). In one of the final sections of the document, "Changing Structures," the bishops resort to generalities about the need to promote policies that confront "racism and its effects in our civic and social institutions" (28). The refusal to name concrete and very specific structures of sin *as* structures of sin (detention centers, prisons) is a significant weakness. Thus, while this document avoids the problems associated with colorblind discourses that purport that race is no longer a relevant reality in American society (racism is, in effect, a thing of the past), it does not rise to the level of an antiracist response, which is what we need.

Although there has been a more concerted effort to confront issues of xenophobia and racism since the Second Vatican Council, the Catholic Church has not lived up to its own name during this period—"catholic" means "universal," so one would expect it to be all-inclusive. What is true of the Catholic Church in general is also true of the works of mercy in particular. There is no explicit mention of racism in official formulations of the works of mercy, and very little, if any, commentary on the relationship between the works of mercy and the sin of racism. The traditional focus of the works of mercy has been on suffering produced by spiritual alienation, material deprivation, and social isolation. It is incumbent on us to reimagine the works of mercy in view of the history of structural racism and, quite specifically, the Catholic Church's own complicity and silence in this history. We stand convinced that the reimagined works of mercy could function as an antiracist politics of mercy. To welcome the stranger and ransom the captive in our world today demands supporting explicitly antiracist initiatives and policies, given the formidable racialization of the immigration and prison industrial complexes. We must focus on the relation between border walls and prisons and between systems that manage social inequalities by expelling and warehousing surplus populations, and we must confront these systems of exclusion as intersecting structural violations of human dignity. Thankfully, there are Catholic organizations like the Jesuit Refugee Service and Homeboy Industries that are doing just this.

Note

1   Bryan Massingale, *Racial Justice and the Catholic Church* (Maryknoll, NY: Orbis, 2010).

CHAPTER 2

Migration

Introduction

On October 3, 2013, a boat carrying over four hundred African migrants began to take on water approximately one-quarter mile off the Italian island of Lampedusa. In an attempt to attract the attention of nearby ships, the passengers aboard the boat set a blanket on fire. The fire immediately spread and engulfed the boat. Some of the migrants jumped into the water, while others quickly moved to the other side of the boat to avoid the flames. This shift in weight distribution caused the boat to capsize. Germani Nagassi, a survivor of the accident, described the scene: "For five hours we were floating, using the dead bodies of our companions ... there is nothing worse than this. There were many children. There was a mother with her four children, a mother with an infant, all lost at sea."[1] Approximately 360 people died off the coast of Lampedusa that day. Lampedusa has been a focal point for the crisis of solidarity in Europe in response to migrants fleeing war-torn, politically unstable, and chronically impoverished countries in Africa. In July 2013, Pope Francis visited Lampedusa on his first official visit outside of Rome after being elected pope in March 2013. By making his first papal visit to Lampedusa, Francis wished to foreground migration as a central area of concern for Catholic life in the twenty-first century.

Closer to the United States, in 2016, Francis celebrated Mass in Ciudad Juárez at the U.S.-Mexican border. He implored onlookers to pray for the "gift of conversion" so that they might shift from policies of violent exclusion to inclusive hospitality: "No more death! No more exploitation! There is still time to change, there is still a way out and a chance, time to implore the mercy of God."[2] The crisis of solidarity in the United States bears some similarities to the European situation but takes on a different form as a result of the unique historical, geographical, and political relationship between the United States and Central America. Still, the stories of the people remain the same: migrants fleeing death-dealing poverty, political instability, persecution, and violence.

On June 26, 2019, an image of the lifeless body of a young man and his baby in the Río Grande at the U.S.-Mexican border caught the world's attention, even provoking comment from Francis. The victims, Óscar Alberto Martínez Ramírez (25 years old) and his daughter Valeria (23 months old), had travelled from El Salvador to escape violence and to seek asylum in the United States. When Ramírez was told that it would take at least two weeks to process the asylum request, he decided to cross the Río Grande with his wife and daughter. He initially took his daughter across the river and arrived safely on the other side. As he turned back to get his wife to take her across the river, Valeria went into the water to follow him. As Martínez turned to try and save his daughter, both were swept away by the current and drowned in the river. The pope expressed great sadness at their deaths and implored the world to join him in "praying for them and for all migrants who have lost their lives while seeking to flee war and misery."[3]

Crisis

The United States is currently in the midst of an immigration-deportation crisis or, to put it more precisely, a crisis of solidarity surrounding migration. During the 2016 presidential election, this issue served as a flashpoint. Donald Trump inveighed against "illegal immigrants," called for a "Muslim ban," and proclaimed that the construction of a wall at the U.S.-Mexican border would be a central focus of his presidency. Furthermore, Trump announced that it would be necessary to build a "deportation force" in order to remove 11 million undocumented immigrants from the United States.[4] Although Trump's rhetoric has been more inflammatory than previous presidents, his record is broadly consistent with his predecessors. Trump is actually on track to deport fewer undocumented immigrants than Presidents G.W. Bush (2 million) and Barack Obama (2.5 million) during their terms in office. The deportation crisis has been building since the late 1990s, following the implementation of the North American Free Trade Agreement (1994) and the Illegal Immigration Reform and Immigration Responsibility Act (1996).[5] It has been estimated that more people have been forcibly removed from the United States in the first eighteen years of the 2000s than the entire prior history of the country.[6]

While the number of those deported has decreased, the number of those detained has increased steadily under the Trump administration as a result of a shift in policy. Whereas the Obama administration focused on the detention and deportation of felons, the Trump administration has expanded the focus to include all undocumented immigrants. As the former acting director of Immigration and Customs Enforcement (ICE), Thomas Homan, testified before Congress in 2017: "If you're in this country illegally and you committed a crime by entering this country, you should be uncomfortable.... You should look over your shoulder, and you need to be worried."[7] The overarching goal of the Trump administration has been to create a climate of fear among undocumented immigrants. Because the U.S. government does not possess the resources to remove all of the estimated eleven million undocumented immigrants in the country, the Trump administration has decided that the most effective means of expelling these populations is to create a climate in which fear of detention and involuntary removal is so extreme that undocumented immigrants view "voluntary" deportation as an act of rational self-interest. In the first eight months of Trump's presidency, ICE arrests increased by 42%, contributing to this climate of fear among undocumented populations.

In April 2018, Attorney General Jeff Sessions ordered prosecutors to adopt a "zero tolerance policy" that would separate families as they attempted to cross the border (although it was subsequently discovered that the process of separating children from their parents had begun a year before this announcement). It is estimated that over 2,400 children were separated from their families from the moment this policy was enacted to its formal conclusion in June 2018. Again, we have an example of the U.S. government attempting to instill fear and terror in a population to deter migrants from crossing the U.S.-Mexican border. The threats of detention, family separation, and deportation serve as the central means by which the Trump administration has attempted to create an atmosphere of terror among migrants.

While this recent episode represents one of the most overtly xenophobic and violent policy positions in recent memory, it stands in continuity with the broader history of American immigration policy. Contrary to the dominant narrative that celebrates an inclusive U.S. immigration policy, with Ellis Island and the Statue of Liberty as its central symbols, we must narrate a more complete history that includes not only Ellis Island, but the Chinese Exclusion Act (1882), the Bracero Program (1942–1964), and countless other policies of racialized exclusion. Even more basically, U.S. history is a history of deportation. Settler colonialism enacted a broad and sweeping displacement of Native Americans, who were expelled (or, in current language, deported) from their land and denied the rights of citizenship in 1776, 1868 (the 14th Amendment), and 1870 (the Naturalization Act). In the aftermath of the Civil War, the category of citizenship was applied to "white(s)" and those of "African nativity or African descent." This same right of citizenship would not be granted to Native Americans and Asians until the 1940s.[8] And it was not until the passage of the Immigration and Nationality Act (1965) that explicit race-based justification for exclusion was eliminated from U.S. immigration law. The United States replaced race-based exclusions with a quota system that permitted 120,000 persons annually from the Western Hemisphere and 170,000 persons from the Eastern Hemisphere to immigrate, irrespective of their race and ethnicity. The 1965 legislation limited immigration to 20,000 persons from any individual country in the Eastern Hemisphere. And in 1976, this 20,000-person limit was applied to the Western Hemisphere as well. Finally, the Immigration Act of 1978 eliminated the quotas based on hemisphere, with a global quota of 290,000 per year and a limit of 20,000 from any one country.

In addition to the racial reasons for the construction of citizenship in U.S. history, American military interventionism abroad has contributed to migrant flows by creating political instability in numerous countries around the world. Of particular importance is the role that U.S. interventionism has played in destabilizing the Central American countries of Guatemala, El Salvador, and Honduras. In 1954 the United States supported a coup that ousted the democratically elected president of Guatemala, Jacobo Árbenz, and helped to install an authoritarian government headed by Carlos Castillo Armas. As a result of the coup and the instability it generated, Guatemala entered into a prolonged civil war (1960–1996) that killed 200,000 Guatemalans. During this period, the United States trained and funded right-wing death squads as a means of outsourcing military activity that served U.S. interests in the region. For example, the United States backed another military coup in Guatemala in 1982 that installed Efraín Ríos Montt as president. In 2013 Ríos Montt was convicted of genocide for his role in attempting to eliminate the indigenous Maya Ixil people. Similar patterns of training and funding of repressive military regimes and supporting military coups can be documented in El Salvador and Honduras. This pattern of interventionism and support for repressive regimes in Guatemala, El Salvador, and Honduras is not solely responsible for the influx of migrants to the United States from these countries. But it does represent a pervasive pattern and long-term, structural reality that has contributed to widespread instability, poverty, and violence in the region.[9]

Economic factors also play a role. The 1994 North American Free Trade Agreement (NAFTA), for example, accelerated migration from Mexico to the United States. Part of the rationale for NAFTA was that it would decelerate such migration. NAFTA was developed to facilitate U.S. capital investment in Mexico, with the stated hope that the Mexican economy would grow, and Mexican workers would be incentivized to stay within the country. In reality, this agreement's more immediate effects include devastating rural Mexican farmers by permitting heavily subsidized American corn to flood the Mexican market. In the two years after the implementation of NAFTA the poverty rate in Mexico jumped from 52% to 69% (thereafter, the poverty rate declined, but given population growth, the absolute number of people in poverty grew steadily). The introduction of cheap American agriculture into Mexico displaced approximately 15 million Mexican farmers from their land. This displacement led to massive waves of migration into Mexican urban centers and into the United States. The end result was that the undocumented population in the United States swelled from 2.2 million before NAFTA to over 11 million by 2005, where it has remained ever since. And this undocumented population, constantly faced with the threat of deportation, suffers from economic exploitation in the United States. Their status as "illegal" forces them to comply with low wages and poor working conditions.

U.S. history is a history of racialized exclusion: settler colonialism, foreign interventionism and alliances with brutal dictatorships (from

Guatemala and Chile to El Salvador and Honduras), and policies that sustain a global order in which the center (the United States) benefits from policies that exploit the periphery (the global South). When U.S. history is narrated in this way, it recasts the entire debate and undermines any attempt to frame the issue as one of simple labels for human beings, either "citizen" or "illegal." Citizenship is a racial construct in U.S. history. Deportation and expulsion have served as potent mechanisms for sustaining the privileges of white citizenship. When it is recognized that migrants have been historically excluded on the basis of their race and ethnicity, that they have been disempowered by free trade agreements and exploitative labor practices, and that they have been displaced by U.S. foreign policy, any attempt to label these persons as "illegal" becomes problematic. Such a term, with its attendant meanings, practices, and social structures, should be rejected—by all, but certainly by Catholics, as we shall now show.

Catholic Social Thought

Anyone who has read the Bible at all closely knows that it is a library of many texts with great variety. What unifies the Christian Bible is a story, running from the beginning to the end of time, of God creating the world, choosing a group of people as God's own (the people of Israel), journeying with that people, supporting them, directing them, correcting them, defining a way of life for them, and eventually blessing all nations through them. (Christians believe that this latter blessing comes in particular through Jesus Christ.) More simply put, the Bible narrates God's accompaniment of people. The story of God's accompaniment of Israel begins with God's creation of human beings in God's image and likeness (Gen 1:26–27); continues with God's election of Abraham and Sarah as father and mother of God's own people (Gen 12–17), eventually called Israel; God's liberation of these people from slavery in Egypt (Exodus) and giving them a Law so that they may be God's holy people (Exodus, Leviticus, Numbers, Deuteronomy); leading them into the land promised to Abraham (Joshua, Judges); residing among them during the monarchy that starts with Saul and passes through the dynasty of David and Solomon (1–2 Samuel, 1–2 Kings); admonishes them for not keeping the Law, eventually allowing God's people to be dispersed and cast into exile (2 Kings, several prophetic books), and then gathering some of them back in the Promised Land (several prophetic books, Ezra, Nehemiah). The story of God's accompaniment of God's people changes, while remaining continuous with the story of Israel, in the New Testament, where through Jesus's life, death, and resurrection it becomes clear that God opens the covenant promised to Abraham even to non-Jews, or Gentiles. God promised Abraham that through his descendants, all nations would be blessed (Gen 12:3, 18:18, 22:18). Peter and Paul preach that this promise has been fulfilled in Jesus (Acts 3:25; Gal 3:8). The Bible's final book, Revelation, envisions a "multitude ... from every nation, race, people, and tongue" at the end of time, gathered in worship before Christ (Rev 7:9). Through this whole grand narrative, God accompanies people, serves as their companion—meaning that God shares life with them ("*com-*" means "with," "*pan*" means "bread"; a companion is the one *with* whom one breaks *bread,* which in numerous world cultures is the source of life). The biblical witness depicts God as companion and recommends practices of companionship to all who believe in this God.

Francis's writings and preaching can help us to understand something important about God's accompaniment of people throughout the Bible and in our world today. God accompanies people *in mercy.* During the 2016 visit to Ciudad Juárez to which we referred earlier, Francis gave a homily on the Book of Jonah.[10] Francis explains how the book tells of a city in peril. God commands the prophet Jonah to travel to Nineveh to warn its people of their coming destruction (Jon 3:4). "Go," God says, "and help them to understand that by the way they treat each other, ordering and organizing themselves, they are only creating death and destruction, suffering and oppression. Make them see this is no way to live, neither for the king nor his subjects, nor for farm fields nor for the cattle. Go and tell them that they have become used to this degrading way of life and have lost their sensitivity to pain." Francis continues: "God sent [Jonah] to testify to what was happening, he sent him to wake up a people intoxicated with themselves." Francis notes that this is how God's mercy operates. Since God's mercy always coordinates with God's justice, often the first way that God shows mercy is by rejecting wickedness—and telling the wicked so. But God's mercy also consists of appealing to people's goodness, the goodness with which God created them. God's mercy operates within people, from their inherent, God-given goodness, to invite them "to see the damage being done at every level." Then God's mercy "pierces evil in order to transform it." This is how God's accompaniment works. It is not neutral co-traveling. It is the consistent and constant operation of mercy that condemns insensitivity to others' pain and works to undo structures that oppress. Francis has in mind as he preaches the crisis of solidarity surrounding migration making itself felt at the U.S.-Mexican border, where countless people suffer, while the United States, like a latter-day Nineveh, has become used to a degrading way of life. God's mercy demands conversion.

The theme of conversion brings us to emphasize something distinctive about God's accompaniment of Israel: God demands that God's people accompany in a special way the widow, the orphan, and the stranger, or the most vulnerable people among them. The last of these is particularly notable for this chapter. It will suffice to return to Deuteronomy, a decisive biblical book for Judaism and Christianity, where God lays the ground for God's accompaniment of God's people, including those actions for which God will bless them, and those for which they will be cursed (Dt 11:26). God "loves the resident alien, giving them food and clothing"; the Law continues, "So you too should love the resident alien, for that is what you were in the land of Egypt" (Dt 10:18–19). This obedience will receive blessing. But "cursed be anyone who deprives the resident alien ... of justice" (Dt 27:19). Such injustice is not tolerated. Conversion must mean, concretely, a turn toward loving the resident alien, the stranger, the migrant.

Theologian and priest Peter Phan has ventured, with the biblical theology of accompaniment in mind, to reexamine the history of the church in terms of migration, so as to make Christians recognize how God has accompanied our church throughout its varied and often tumultuous history, and to encourage the people of the church to commit themselves to accompanying today's migrants with mercy. Phan even contends that "Migration is a permanent feature of the church, and not just a historical phenomenon."[11] In saying this he translates into newer terms a slightly older insight about the church from the twentieth century: that the church's condition on earth is a pilgrimage. The **pilgrim church**, as the Second Vatican Council's Dogmatic Constitution on the Church, *Lumen Gentium*, calls it (*LG*, 7), travels through this world waiting for its fulfillment at the end of time in heaven. Phan points out that this insight needs to be filled out. The church's travel through time has not just been toward heaven. Instead, it has carried the church, God's people, all over the globe.

Phan discusses eight migrations that have marked church history. We shall not provide the detail he does, but it is worth listing these.

- The Jewish-Christian diaspora in the aftermath of the destruction of the Temple in Jerusalem in 70 CE.
- The Christian exodus from Palestine into Syria, Greece, the western Mediterranean, North Africa (especially Egypt), and Asia (especially India) in the second century.
- The transfer of the church's geographical center to Constantinople in the fourth century, which decisively shaped the Byzantine and Orthodox churches for centuries to come, involving widespread migrations both forced and voluntary.
- The movement of Germanic Christian tribes throughout Europe during the Middle Ages.
- The so-called Age of Discovery (1492 forward), when Latin American churches were developed, and the face of the Asian churches changed with European missions and conquests.
- The period of modernization (1650–1918), with the colonization of Latin America, Asia, and Africa, the forced migrations of the slave trade, and other economic ventures, all of which implicated the church in a variety of ways.
- After World War II (1945 forward), decolonization and a variety of other social factors brought refugees, asylum seekers, and other migrants around the world; in many cases, these people were Christians; in others, Christians were affected by receiving migrants into their communities.
- In the opening decades of the twenty-first century, wars in the Middle East ravaged ancient Christian churches, and economic globalization displaced people by the millions; the Catholic Church is now truly "catholic," universal, and global.

The point of Phan's historical narrative is that the church has always been on the move, from its earliest days to its latest—and God has remained with the church throughout this migratory history. His focus on the *church's* migration underscores a positive reason why Catholics should be hospitable to migrants: our church, which is the universal church, has always led a migrant condition. This should lead Catholics to sympathize with migrants of all sorts, whether "inside" the church or "outside." We all share a pilgrim condition, and we all can hope that God will accompany us throughout our travails; in this, we must faithfully imitate our God.

It is critical that the church's remembrance is not only of its own positive history of migration, but also the participation of its members in political projects of exclusion. Specifically, this means that Catholics are called to remember their countries' own histories and the debts and obligations that flow from past wrongs into the present. Catholic memory involves a dual structure: remembering past faults and retrieving elements from the Catholic tradition to take responsibility for these faults and to build a more inclusive and just future.

The Politics of Mercy

The politics of mercy as it applies to the crisis of solidarity surrounding migration focuses on three spiritual works of mercy: **admonishing the sinner**, **forgiving offenses**, and **bearing wrongs patiently**; as well as one corporal work of mercy, **welcoming the stranger**, which is also known as **harboring the harborless**—a potent image, given that we began this chapter with stories of migrants drowning. The spiritual works of mercy pertain primarily to the need for reconciliation with God. The unwillingness of nations like the United States to welcome strangers and harbor the harborless is a grave sin, a breach of communion that cries out to heaven, and that demands dramatic conversion. Welcoming the stranger in twenty-first-century America demands direct action to resist expulsion of migrants and to provide sanctuary for them, along with efforts to transform society to be more hospitable across the board.

Spiritual Works of Mercy: Reconciliation

As we saw James Keenan doing with the three spiritual works of mercy that train people in being vigilant (Chapter 1), so does he group three more spiritual works of mercy because they help people to develop the habit of appreciating their need for reconciliation with God.[12] These three spiritual works are admonishing sinners, forgiving offenses, and bearing wrongs patiently. Obviously, all of these can and should be directed toward others, which would involve me pointing out to others where they have gone wrong, offering forgiveness in response to those who have offended me, and patiently enduring such offenses, inasmuch as I can. (Keenan notes that, for example, survivors of abuse should not be advised to "bear wrongs patiently.") But beyond these obvious applications, Keenan indicates that these spiritual works of mercy demand something more of their practitioners. This "something more" is what we want to focus on, as we think about a spirituality that could help to build up a politics of mercy.

The spiritual works of admonishing, forgiving, and bearing wrongs patiently demand that the one who practices them recognize *his own* need to be warned against sinning, to be forgiven, and to be borne with patience. In short, these spiritual works help their practitioner to know himself as a sinner, as one out of step or even out of touch with God. Any Catholic work of identifying, criticizing, resisting, or building alternatives to the current racialized, expulsive system of mass deportation in the United States of America should have as its impetus recognition of the need for restored communion with God, which will reinvigorate love of neighbor.

Such a recognition is particularly important with regard to the crisis we are examining in this chapter. Keenan suggests that if the spiritual works of mercy that habituate people into appreciating their need for reconciliation with God teach us anything, it is not to assume a stance of moral superiority (over the sinners one admonishes, those one forgives, and those whose wrongs one bears patiently). Combating moral superiority proves crucial with regard to the crisis of solidarity surrounding migration. In the United States, it has become a nationwide habit to pontificate about the need for migrants to "come here legally" or to "follow the proper process." U.S. citizens often assume a position of moral superiority: they follow laws and expect others to do so as well. But we know from our consideration of the crisis that not only is such an air of moral superiority imprecise; it may also be completely unfounded or based on historical inaccuracies (such as "my ancestors arrived here legally"). Furthermore, it has racial overtones that must be judged entirely unacceptable by the standard of Catholic spirituality.

Keenan explains that these three spiritual works of mercy should develop in their practitioners a "reconciling spirit." We see them as cultivating a spirituality of accompaniment. Such a spirituality responds in kind to a God who accompanies us and travels our life journey with us, supporting us all the way (Mt 28:20), even in our sin (Rom 4:25; 1 Pet 2:24; see Is 53:5), even unto death (Phil 2:8; see Is 53:12) and beyond (1 Pet 3:19), as God works within us and around us to welcome us toward the heavenly home prepared for us (Jn 14:2–3; 1 Cor 2:9). We have already learned that there are resources in Catholic theology for seeing God as the one who accompanies us and that seeing God in this way can propel Catholic action for solidarity with migrants. We have also discussed how the church's history as pilgrim and migrant should prompt us to reassess how we as individuals and how the social groups we belong to treat migrants, and to pressure society to treat them better. What we have added here is that the self-examination involved in admonishing, forgiving, and bearing wrongs patiently can lend greater spiritual depth to these actions. This spirituality demands conversion: a new heart that trades moral, legal, and racial superiority for a humble spirit of welcoming solidarity.

Charity: Welcome the Stranger

Catholics should not forget that Jesus and his earliest followers were regarded as foreigners, alien to the great urban center of Jerusalem (e.g., Mk 14:70; Mt 26:73; Lk 22:59; Acts 2:7). Furthermore, in the Book of Exodus, God instructs the people of Israel: "Do not oppress the foreigner; you yourselves know how it feels to be foreigners, because you were foreigners in Egypt" (Ex 23:9). Even more ominously, Jesus describes the fate of someone who was inhospitable to the stranger in the final judgment scene of the Gospel of Matthew (Mt 25:43). Early Christian theologians such as Cyprian, Tertullian, and Clement urged their fellow Christians to practice the hospitality of welcoming and sheltering strangers.

Perhaps the most prominent Catholic tradition of welcoming strangers is the Benedictine tradition, following St. Benedict of Nursia's counsel that "all guests who arrive be received as Christ, because He will say: 'I was a stranger and you took Me in' (Mt 25:35)."[13] Francis has invoked this tradition in his own teaching on hospitality to migrants: "the encounter with the other ... is also an encounter with Christ," because Christ is the one "with ragged clothes, dirty feet, agonized faces, sore bodies, unable to speak our language."[14] If Catholics remember this tradition of hospitality, they should be scandalized to discover that the current era has forced numerous populations to migrate from their homes, only to be met where they arrive with widespread, vitriolic anti-immigrant animus. From a Catholic theological point of view, steeped in the same imagination as St. Benedict, rather than being viewed as "illegal," migrants should be viewed as Christ, as opportunities to love another as Christ and to welcome Christ as Christ has welcomed us (1 Jn 4:12 and Jn 13:34–35; Rom 15:7).

When our engagement with the crisis of solidarity in relation to migrants and the threat of mass deportation is guided by the narration of U.S. history, the Catholic Church's own history of migration, and the history of the corporal work of mercy of welcoming the stranger, it follows that the Catholic response today should be to build a social order in which no person is branded as illegal and the threat of deportation is eliminated once and for all for the approximately 11 million undocumented migrants who currently reside in the United States. Obviously, we are today in the midst of the opposite of this vision, one in which the term "illegal" is employed by politicians and citizens alike to marginalize vulnerable racialized groups in America. So what is to be done?

Catholics should support local, grassroots experiments in **inclusive hospitality**. Concretely, the most significant embodied and political act of the church that would flow from an honest engagement with the United States' history of racist exclusion is the practice of **sanctuary**. The practice of church sanctuary emerged in the 1980s in response to the influx of Central American migrants, particularly Salvadorans and Guatemalans, during the civil wars then consuming the region. In response to the failure of civil authorities to provide legal refuge for these migrants (only 2.6% of Salvadorans and 1.8% of Guatemalans were granted formal refugee status), sanctuary churches (whose numbers swelled to nearly 150 congregations in the mid-1980s) emerged as spaces of hospitality and protection. The Department of Justice under Ronald Reagan responded to this practice by criminalizing those providing sanctuary and by prosecuting several activists associated with the movement. The indictment of these activists accused them of running a "modern-day underground railroad that smuggled Central American natives across the Mexican border with Arizona." Remarkably, the indictment links the work of the sanctuary churches to the work of the Underground Railroad, which provided asylum for former slaves as they escaped the manifestly immoral and unjust laws of the time—and, scandalously, this association seems to be taken as a negative.

While this initial form of sanctuary practice faded with the end of the civil wars in Central America in the early 1990s, a "new" sanctuary movement emerged in response to reforms in immigration policy in the 2000s. Specifically, in March of 2006, Cardinal Roger Mahony, the Archbishop of Los Angeles, instructed the clergy in his diocese to disregard the specific provisions of the congressional Border Protection, Terrorism, and Illegal Immigration Control Act of 2005, which criminalized the act of giving aid or humanitarian assistance without checking the legal status of the recipient. The subsequent battle between the Catholic Church, joined by other Christian congregations, and the Congress led to the organization of the new sanctuary movement. At this time (2019), numerous local Catholic parishes serve as sanctuary churches.

Justice: A Sanctuary Politics

To pursue justice for migrants is to reflect on what this church practice of sanctuary means for restructuring the whole of society. The question becomes: what does a **sanctuary politics** look like in response to the current crisis? The response should be multifaceted. It must involve a critique of the punitive features of current immigration and deportation policy while simultaneously describing reforms necessary to build a society in which the detainment, punishment, and deportation of migrants is no longer the default response to migrants. Let us highlight three specific facets of a sanctuary politics. First, it necessarily entails a reckoning with U.S. interventionist foreign policy and its role in destabilizing the Central American region countless times over the past century (not to mention the Middle East, with Afghanistan, Iraq, and now Syria). Of course, blowback from American foreign policy in the region is not the exclusive cause of migration, but it has played a pivotal role. This is evidenced by the recent influx of migrants from Honduras, Guatemala, and El Salvador—as noted above, all Central American countries that have experienced sustained periods of political destabilization in the wake of American-supported coups d'état or American-enabled civil wars.[15] Second, and consistent with the suggestions made in Chapter 1 for transforming economic policy in a more distributive direction, it is critical that Catholics advocate for more equitable trade policies and the protection of the labor rights of the undocumented. Third, it involves pointing to the contingency of border construction to illuminate the possibility of a different configuration. There has to be a critique of the binary that forces us to choose between "border security" and "open borders." This way of framing the available options is incomplete and provides cover for punitive "law-and-order" policies. Perhaps most importantly, this framing staves off pressure for economic reforms that would improve migrants' actual, material conditions.

Advocating for a shift in the approach of U.S. Customs and Border Protection from policing, separating families, and expelling migrants to humanitarian ends of providing relief and protection for them should be seen as a critical front in the attempt to build a politics of sanctuary in the United States. A holistic sanctuary politics would aim to protect the rights of the stranger who bears the face of Christ by resisting the view that anyone should be labelled "illegal." The opposite of a politics of ever-more-militarized border security is quite clearly a politics of sanctuary. The politics of sanctuary bases itself in a vision of freedom. Real freedom is not freedom *from* dangers, real or imagined, but freedom *for* enacting a merciful ethos of accompaniment. The fact of the matter is that if the Catholic Church fails to embody a radical sanctuary politics, thus living out concretely its Christ-given mission of mercy, we have little hope that the United States will move in this direction. The Catholic Church is the largest single religious group in the United States, and it has witnessed only episodically to a sanctuary politics. In a recent poll, 45% of white Catholics responded that the country has no responsibility to welcome refugees. (A remarkable 68% of white evangelicals registered the same opinion.) If the politics of mercy could become more consistent and widespread, a cultural revolution could be accomplished. This would especially be the case if the Catholic Church could join with other Christian churches as companions on our shared pilgrim journey.

We keep this account of the politics of mercy brief, because we believe that the best way to illustrate it is with the example of a worldwide Catholic organization that is attempting to enact a global politics of mercy addressed to the crisis of solidarity surrounding migration. Thus we now consider the Jesuit Refugee Service.

Conclusion: Jesuit Refugee Service

In 1979 Pedro Arrupe, the Superior General of the Jesuits, witnessed with horror the plight of the Vietnamese boat people as they fled the instability and violence of Vietnam after the end of the war in 1975. In response, Arrupe reached out to 50 Jesuit leaders around the world to begin the process of discerning how to respond to the plight of refugees. The Jesuits convened an international meeting in 1980 and soon after announced that working with refugees would serve as a new apostolate for the order. As a result, the Jesuit Refugee Service (JRS) was born, and shortly thereafter the first site, Astalli Center, opened in Rome in 1981 in the basement of a Jesuit community. Astalli continues to respond to the material and spiritual needs of refugees who have fled persecution and violence in their native countries.

From the outset, JRS was imagined as an apostolate that sought to provide an integrated approach that was responsive to both the material and spiritual needs of migrants and refugees. In 1980, Arrupe observed that "the help needed is not only material: in a special way the Society is being called to render a service that is human, pedagogical, and spiritual."[16] Thus, the Charter Statement for JRS (2000) described its mission in terms of its commitment to **accompany**, **serve**, and **defend** (later changed to **advocate**) migrants and refugees.[17]

The practice of **accompaniment** is central to JRS's approach to its ministry to migrants, just as it has been central to the way in which God has related to God's people throughout history.[18] The Jesuits are often referred to as "companions of Jesus," and, in view of Jesus's instruction in Matthew 25, the Jesuit Order has recognized that to be a companion of Jesus is to be a companion of the poor, the outcast, and the stranger.[19] Importantly, JRS has viewed its work as "being with" and "doing with" and not simply "doing for." Arrupe's successor, Peter Hans Kolvenbach, SJ, describes JRS's ministry of accompaniment:

> We want our presence among refugees to be one of sharing with them, of accompaniment, of walking together along the same path. In so far as possible, we want to feel what they have felt, suffer as they have, share the same hopes and aspirations, see the world through their eyes. We ourselves would like to become one with the refugees and displaced people so that, all together, we can begin the search for a new life.[20]

JRS seeks to be a companion of migrants and refugees by being with them in refugee camps, detention centers, and conflict zones.[21] Accompaniment is foundational to the work of JRS because it supports a personalist approach to service and advocacy by viewing migrants and refugees as active agents and participants in the work of building a more inclusive and just social order.

The practice of **service** seeks to offer direct humanitarian aid to migrants and refugees through livelihood programs, psychosocial services to promote healing and psychological well-being, and educational opportunities to migrants and refugees in camps and temporary settlements where formal educational opportunities often do not exist. Recently, for example, JRS has partnered with Jesuit colleges and universities in the United States to offer higher education courses to global migrants.[22] Jesuit Worldwide Learning: Higher Education at the Margins (JWL-HEM) offers a fully accredited online diploma in Liberal Studies and a number of Community Service Learning tracks that are tailored to the needs of local communities.[23]

The practice of **advocacy** requires seeking structural remedies to the plight of migrants and refugees. Thus, in addition to the work of spiritual accompaniment and offering direct humanitarian, educational, and psychosocial services, JRS views its mission as promoting and defending the rights of migrants and refugees. Advocacy takes on a number of different forms in JRS. At the international level, JRS offices in Rome, Geneva, and Brussels present the concerns of local JRS sites to international organizations like the United Nations and the International Organization on Migration in order to "enhance international cooperation in sharing responsibility for protecting them."[24] Additionally, JRS provides legal assistance and supports refugees as they file asylum claims. This is absolutely critical work because migrants and refugees rarely have the resources to navigate the complexities of legal frameworks from host countries in foreign languages. Finally, JRS aims to uphold a more humane perception of migrants and refugees in the general public by supporting programs that seek **reconciliation** among different ethnic, religious, and racial groups. Migrants and refugees fleeing the instability and violence of their native countries are often subjected not only to harsh forms of material deprivation, but also to racist and xenophobic attacks from citizens in their host countries. To counteract the rise of xenophobia and racism in European countries, the United States, and elsewhere, JRS has made the work of reconciliation a strategic priority. It defines "reconciliation" as the attempt to "create right relationships" between refugees and their host communities. For example, JRS Europe initiated a program entitled "I Get You" that sought to identify Community Building Initiatives (CBIs) that could bring together local citizens and refugees.[25] The result was that nine different European countries hosted a variety of local events (football matches, community gardening projects, and international food festivals) that brought together refugees and citizens from the local community. The aim of this program is consonant with Francis's call for a "culture of encounter." Francis has argued that when we spend time with others, begin to understand their stories, and develop relationships with people and communities different from our own, it becomes more difficult to scapegoat them or to be indifferent toward their suffering.

Overall, JRS provides services in 56 countries and serves over 677,000 people (55% of whom are Muslim).[26] In 2018, 1% of refugees worldwide were served by JRS: 236,839 migrants through JRS education programs, 54,789 migrants through JRS advocacy programs, and 16,657 migrants through JRS livelihood programs.[27]

In relation to the focus of this chapter, JRS offers programs in Mexico and the United States that seek to respond to the needs of Central American migrants and refugees. In Mexico, JRS responded to the recent (2018–2019) caravans of migrants traveling from Honduras, El Salvador, and Guatemala to the United States by offering legal support to help these migrants process their asylum claims. JRS also offered direct aid and psychosocial support in Tapachula, Mexico, where many had been placed by Mexican authorities.[28] In 2018, JRS Mexico accompanied 4,662 migrants in Tapachula by offering them psychosocial and legal support. Additionally, in the United States, JRS created the Detention Chaplaincy Program to respond to the spiritual needs of migrants detained by the Department of Homeland Security. Chaplains and lay volunteers offer Mass and ecumenical services to support the spiritual needs of the detained from all faith traditions. In 2017, JRS staff in five adult detention centers offered 1,388 religious services, 1,350 religious teachings, and 1,392 spiritual support sessions to minister to the needs of over 11,000 detainees. The work of the JRS in Mexico and the United States enacts a politics of mercy that connects direct humanitarian assistance and spiritual accompaniment to long-term, justice-oriented projects that advocate for the legal rights of migrants.

Francis was elected pope in March 2013. In September of that year, he visited Astalli Center in Rome to highlight the importance of JRS as a response to the crisis of solidarity surrounding the growing number of global migrants.[29] In a message sent to the community of Astalli on its 35th anniversary in 2016, Francis observed that the work done by JRS represents a courageous witness to the fact that every migrant and refugee "who knocks on the door bears the face of God, the flesh of Christ."[30]

Notes

1   Sarah Stillman, "Lampedusa's Migrant Tragedy, and Ours," *The New Yorker*, October 10, 2013, https://www.newyorker.com/news/daily-comment/lampedusas-migrant -tragedy-and-ours.

2   Pope Francis, "Homily of His Holiness, Pope Francis (Ciudad Juárez Fairgrounds)," February 17, 2016, https://w2.vatican.va/content/francesco/en/homilies/2016/ documents/papa-francesco_20160217_omelia-messico-ciudad-jaurez.html.

3   Vatican News, "Pope Saddened by Death," June 2019, https://www.vaticannews. va/en/pope/news/2019-06/pope-sorrow-death-migrants-death-united- states-mexico-border.html.

4   David Nakamura, "Trump Administration Moving Quickly to Build Up Nationwide Deportation Force," *Washington Post*, April 12, 2017, https://www. washingtonpost.com/politics/trump-administration-moving-quickly-to- build-up-nationwide-deportation-force/2017/04/12/7a7f59c2-1f87-11e7- be2a-3a1fb24d4671_story.html.

5   Dara Lind, "The Disastrous, Forgotten 1996 Law that Created Today's Immigration Problem," *Vox*, April 28, 2016, https://www.vox.com/2016/4/28/11515132/ iirira-clinton-immigration.

6   Tanya Golash-Boza, *Deported: Immigrant Policing, Disposable Labor, and Global Capitalism* (New York: New York University Press, 2015). Golash-Boza observes that by 2014, six years into Obama's presidency, his administration had deported more undocumented immigrants—two million—than the total of deportations prior to 1997. Golash-Boza, "The Parallels between Mass Incarceration and Mass Deportation: An Intersectional Analysis of State Repression," *Journal of World Systems Research* 22, no. 2 (2016): 484–509, 485.

7   Maria Sacchetti, "ICE Chief Tells Lawmakers Agency Needs Much More Money for Immigration Arrests," *Washington Post*, June 13, 2017, https://www .washingtonpost.com/local/social-issues/ice-chief-tells-lawmakers-agency- needs-much-more-money-for-immigration-arrests/2017/06/13/86651e86- 5054-11e7-b064-828ba60fbb98_story.html.

8   Aviva Chomsky, *They Take Our Jobs! And 20 Other Myths about Immigration* (Boston, MA: Beacon Press, 2018), 87.

9   Lisa Marie Cacho, *Social Death: Racialized Rightlessness and the Criminalization of the Unprotected* (New York: New York University Press, 2012), 123; see also Mark Weisbrot, Stephan Lefebvre, and Joseph Sammut, "Did NAFTA Help Mexico?: An Assessment after 20 Years," Center for Economic and Policy Research, February 2014.

10   Pope Francis, "Homily of His Holiness Pope Francis (Ciudad Juárez Fairgrounds)."

11   Peter C. Phan, "*Deus Migrator*—God the Migrant: Migration of Theology and Theology of Migration," *Theological Studies* 77, no. 4 (2016): 845–68, 866. Material in the next few paragraphs comes from this same article.

12   James F. Keenan, SJ, *The Works of Mercy: The Heart of Catholicism,* 3rd ed. (Lanham, MD: Rowman & Littlefield, 2017), 65–69.

13   Saint Benedict, *The Rule of St. Benedict*, ed. by Timothy Frye, Timothy Horner, and Imogene Baker (Collegeville, MN: Liturgical Press, 1981).

14   Vatican News, "Pope at Mass: Be Free from Fear of Migrants and Refugees," https://www.vaticannews.va/en/pope/news/2019-02/pope-francis-mass- sacrofano-migrants-refugees.html.

15   On this, see Stephen Kinzer, *Overthrow: America's Century of Regime Change from Hawaii to Iraq* (New York: Times Books, 2007).

16   Pedro Arrupe, SJ, "The Society of Jesus and the Refugee Problem," November 14, 1980, http://www.jrsusa.org/Assets/Sections/Downloads/ArrupeLetter.pdf.

17   Jesuit Refugee Service, "The Charter of Jesuit Refugee Service," https://jrsap .org/Assets/Sections/Downloads/char-en21.pdf.

18   Kevin O'Brien, SJ, "Consolation in Action: The Jesuit Refugee Service and the Ministry of Accompaniment," *Studies in Jesuit Spirituality* 37, no. 4 (2015): 1-51;

Kevin Ahern, "The Justice Legacy of *Populorum Progressio*: A Jesuit Case Study," *Journal of Moral Theology*, 6 no. 1 (2017): 39–56, and *Structures of Grace: Catholic Organizations Serving the Common Good* (Maryknoll, NY: Orbis Books, 2015).

19 Ahern, *Structures of Grace*, 50.

20 Peter-Hans Kolvenbach, "Review of the Jesuit Refugee Service," A Letter to the Society of Jesus, February 14, 1990.

21 Jesuit Refugee Service East Africa, "Accompaniment," http://www.jrsea.org/accompaniment.

22 See Ahern, *Structures of Grace*, 52–53.

23 See the website for Jesuit Worldwide Learning: https://www.jwl.org/en/home.

24 Jesuit Refugee Service, "Advocacy," https://jrs.net/en/programme/advocacy/.

25 Jesuit Refugee Service Europe, "I Get You," https://jrseurope.org/assets/Regions/EUR/media/files/JRS_Europe_igetyou_full.pdf.

26 Thomas Reese, "Jesuit Refugee Service: Accompanying, Serving, Advocating," *National Catholic Reporter*, October 6, 2016, https://www.ncronline.org/blogs/faith-and-justice/jrs-accompanying-serving-and-advocating-refugees.

27 Jesuit Refugee Service, "Our Impact," https://jrs.net/en/our-work/our-impact/.

28 Jesuit Refugee Service, "JRS—2018 Annual Report," https://jrs.net/wp-content/uploads/2019/06/JRS-2018-annual-report.pdf.

29 Pope Francis, "Address of Holy Father to 'Astalli Centre.'" September 9, 2013, http://w2.vatican.va/content/francesco/en/speeches/2013/september/documents/papa-francesco_20130910_centro-astalli.html.

30 Pope Francis, "Message on the Occasion of the 35th Anniversary of the Centro Astalli," April 19, 2016, https://w2.vatican.va/content/francesco/en/messages/pont-messages/2016/documents/papa-francesco_20160419_videomessaggio-centro-astalli-35anniv.html.

CHAPTER 3

Mass Incarceration

Introduction

T HE YEAR 2019 MARKS the twenty-fifth anniversary of the Violent Crime Control and Law Enforcement Act of 1994. Democratic president Bill Clinton passed this legislation with the support of a Republican majority in Congress. Among its chief aims was to place mandatory minimum sentences on persons convicted of three felony offenses.[1] While mass incarceration predates this policy, critics of mass incarceration point to this type of legislation as a central mechanism that has led to the dramatic expansion of the prison system over the past forty years. The rationale offered in defense of this policy is that a person who has committed a third felony offense is, in some very real sense, beyond rehabilitation and should be imprisoned for life to protect society from him or her.

Curtis Wilkerson is a victim of this policy in the state of California.[2] In 1995 Wilkerson walked into a store and stole a single pair of ordinary white socks worth $2.50. He was caught by security guards and arrested for the theft. Wilkerson was thirty-three years old at the time. His last encounter with law enforcement had been in 1981, when as a teenager he was convicted twice for "abetting robbery" by serving as a "lookout." For those offenses he was sentenced to six years in jail. After serving the sentence, Wilkerson found a job as a forklift driver and successfully put his life back together. In 1995, Wilkerson was charged with a felony for the above-mentioned theft of socks (this is usually prosecuted as a misdemeanor offense; Wilkerson's race likely played a role in the prosecution's pursuit of a felony charge). This felony was his third and triggered the California "three strikes" law, which meant that Wilkerson was sentenced to 25 years to life in prison for the theft of a single pair of socks. Wilkerson had not committed a violent crime and did not represent a serious threat to society. But the three-strikes policy viewed him as beyond rehabilitation and a threat to be managed by the carceral system in the United States.

In California, where Wilkerson resides, there are over 4,000 prisoners serving life sentences for nonviolent crimes because of three-strikes legislation. A racial disparity exists among those sentenced as a result of this legislation. African Americans make up roughly 7% of California's population. But African Americans comprise 28% of the California state prison population and 45% of those sentenced because of the three-strikes legislation. Such legislation is one piece of a broader constellation of laws and policies that have led to the reality of mass incarceration. The widespread incarceration of individuals in the United States is an issue in and of itself, but its disproportionate impact on communities of color makes this a central concern of a Catholic antiracist politics of mercy.

Crisis

In 1980 the prison population in the United States was approximately 300,000 people. By the 1990s that figure had grown to almost 1 million, and by the 2000s it had reached 2.4 million people. Presently, one in thirty-five adults in the United States is in prison, on parole, or on probation.[3] The United States accounts for approximately 5% of the global population but warehouses 25% of the global prison population. These statistics are jarring and raise a number of disquieting questions about the rapid development of the United States' vast carceral apparatus.

The persistence of structural racism in American history is often identified as the primary cause of the rise of mass incarceration in the United States. Michelle Alexander offers the most famous example of this approach in *The New Jim Crow: Mass Incarceration in an Age of Colorblindness* (2012). Her book describes how mass incarceration succeeded Jim Crow policies as a new means of social control of African American populations. She contends that after the Civil Rights

Act of 1964 there emerged a political backlash by disaffected whites who feared that their jobs, educational access, and social standing were threatened by the social transformations associated with the Civil Rights Movement. The Republican Party saw this disaffection as an opportunity for electoral advantage and seized upon it. They successfully deployed the so-called Southern Strategy, a prime example of strategic racism, that utilized coded forms of racism to appeal to whites' racial resentments. After the Civil Rights Movement it was no longer socially acceptable to use explicit forms of racism in public, so politicians employed "dog whistles" to signal to voters that their policies would serve white interests and punish communities of color. [4] Richard Nixon, Ronald Reagan, George H.W. Bush, and Bill Clinton all built a winning electoral strategy around policy proposals to cut welfare, enact a war on drugs, and get tough on crime. As politicians achieved electoral success through dog-whistle strategies, they attempted to deliver on their campaign promises by passing legislation that launched the war on drugs and tough-on-crime policies that swept unprecedented numbers of African American men into the criminal justice system. Alexander surveys the results: "more African American adults are under correctional control today—in prison or jail, on probation or parole—than were enslaved in 1850, a decade before the Civil War began."[5]

Alexander argues that the exploitation of racial resentment by politicians propelled the rise of mass incarceration. It is little wonder, therefore, that the project has targeted African American and Latino populations and produced astonishing results: people of color comprise 37% of the U.S. population but 67% of the prison population. Furthermore, African American men are nearly six times as likely to be incarcerated as white men, and Latinos are nearly two times as likely as white men to be incarcerated. A number of factors contribute to the disproportionate number of persons of color incarcerated in comparison to their white counterparts. Among them are the following: structural disadvantages due to the history of racism in the United States, the concentration of poverty among communities of color, implicit bias in policing communities of color, and sentencing disparity in the criminal justice system. Independent of the specific reasons for the racial disparity, the rise of mass incarceration has been propelled by a dramatic increase in the imprisonment of persons of color.

Alexander observes that the effect of this project has been to restore Jim Crow forms of "legal discrimination" in the African American community: voter disenfranchisement, exclusion from public assistance (welfare) and public housing benefits, and exclusion from employment and educational opportunities. This restriction of rights and of access to public goods is a form of **civil death**. Alexander's argument is that once a person is labelled a "felon," forms of discrimination that have been legislatively outlawed can be reinstated. Thus, where the Jim Crow system was explicit in its racist rationale for discrimination, the system of mass incarceration carries this discrimination forward as a **colorblind** project that now excludes on the basis of "criminality" rather than "race." According to Alexander, this new system functions as a continuation of the old Jim Crow because criminalization and incarceration disproportionately affect persons of color. While the rationale for discrimination has shifted, the material effect remains the same: civil death for formerly incarcerated persons of color.

Civil death is one feature of the exclusionary effects of incarceration. On another level, the effect of incarceration is **social death**. Orlando Patterson coined this term in relation to the social institution of slavery in *Slavery and Social Death*.[6] He argued that slavery spelled social death in three ways for the enslaved: systemic violence, generalized humiliation, and "natal" alienation (that is, alienation from ancestors and children). In *Prison and Social Death*, Jason Price reveals how the project of mass incarceration extends slavery's project of inflicting social death on those persons deemed nonentities by racist structures in society.[7] Social death is a permanent condition that expands beyond the legal realm ("civil death"). Social death entails systemic alienation from family and community, physical deprivation and isolation from others, and loss of social standing. This distinction between civil death and social death is important. Even if it were possible to restore legal rights to the formerly incarcerated, isolation and stigmatization would persist. The project of restoring social life to those who have been condemned to social death necessitates a deeper transformation of the way in which formerly incarcerated persons are integrated into society.

The U.S. prison system is an apparatus that leads to civil and social death for the incarcerated. From a Catholic perspective, we should question whether a punitive, death-dealing approach to social problems is adequate. In the sections that follow we explore a Catholic alternative that seeks not punishment and social death for the incarcerated but restorative justice and inclusion at the Lord's Table for those labelled "criminals."

Catholic Social Thought

The dominant approach to criminal justice proceeds by asking who committed the crime and how should that person be punished. This **retributive** approach seeks to impose a punishment that will cause some form of suffering in the offender as payment for criminal activity. This retributive model is the common-sense understanding of criminal justice in the United States. If someone commits a criminal act, particularly if it harms others, he or she owes a debt to society that can only be paid by undergoing some form of physical, psychological, and social suffering. Incarceration constitutes the primary form of retributive justice within the American criminal justice system.

The Catholic tradition advocates for an alternative approach rooted in a commitment to restoration rather than retribution and punishment. **Restorative justice** seeks to repair the harm done to members of the community as a result of a criminal act. This model of justice was endorsed two decades ago by the United States Conference of Catholic Bishops (USCCB). The bishops followed the prophetic words and work of Pope John Paul II, who opposed the death penalty and who prompted people to envision "a system of penal justice ever more in line with human dignity and thus, in the end, with God's plan for man and society" (*EV*, 56).[8] In their document on crime and justice, *Responsibility, Rehabilitation, and Restoration: A Catholic Perspective on Crime and Criminal Justice* (2000), the USCCB set forth several goals for reforming the criminal justice system that would align it with the restorative model for justice.[9] Among the recommendations they make are the following:

- The primary goal for addressing crime should be fostering healthy community. This would begin, as is consistent with the restorative justice model, by taking into account the harm done to victims and communities.

- Punishment can never be pursued for its own sake, but rather as part of an effort to correct, to treat, to restore, and to heal not just the victims of crimes, but offenders as well. Punishment must be constructive and rehabilitative, with prisoners being challenged to turn their lives around.
- Efforts to reform criminal justice must begin with the recognition of the role that economic inequality and racism play in contributing to crime and shaping attitudes toward crime and criminal justice. Thus measures like fighting child poverty, educating people, and supporting families should be adopted as anti-crime strategies.
- For-profit prisons must be categorically opposed.
- Once released from jail and prison, ex-offenders must be welcomed back into society as full, participating members (to the extent feasible), and their right to vote should be supported.
- Consistent with the first priority they set, the bishops insist that crime must be placed in a community context and coordinated with efforts to empower communities to restore a sense of security.

In this way the bishops attempt to provide the ingredients for an alternative to a retributive criminal justice system that, even 20 years ago, was wreaking havoc on communities, especially poor communities of color, across the United States.

The USCCB's case for restorative justice has its theological roots in the **Paschal Mystery** of Jesus Christ. "Paschal Mystery" means the saving reality of Jesus's suffering, death, and resurrection, which puts on full display the meaning of his whole life and ministry. It is the central term in **soteriology**, or the Christian theology of salvation, which accounts for what it means to be "saved" and what it means to profess faith in Christ as savior. A politics of mercy, which we talk about in the next section, should have substantial soteriological grounding in the Paschal Mystery.

Jesus's way of life led him to the cross, as the overall plot of all four Gospels shows. His ministry of healing (Mk 3:10), forgiveness of sin (Mt 9:2), reconciliation (even among enemies, as with Herod and Pilate, Lk 23:12), and preaching God's peace (Jn 14:27) provoked a violent reaction from the religious and political authorities of his time. Jesus was arrested as an outlaw (Mt 26:55). He was tried and, though found guilty of no crime, executed as a criminal alongside other criminals (Lk 23:33). Upon his death, it would have seemed that Jesus was yet another misguided religious insurrectionist who had overstepped his bounds and been snuffed out by the normal operation of this world's powers—that is, to cast out and kill all those who appear to threaten the normal and decent functioning of society. Caiaphas, the high priest, expresses this operation of worldly power succinctly: "It is better that one man die instead of the people, so that the whole nation may not perish" (Jn 11:50). Jesus was killed to keep the peace, to retain business as usual, and to discourage others from disrupting it like he did.

But the crux of the Paschal Mystery is found in what came after Jesus's death. God raised him from the dead, "releasing him from the throes of death, because it was impossible for him to be held by it" (Acts 2:24). This statement by Peter at Pentecost is worth our reflection. He argues that Jesus, precisely as the one who healed, forgave sin, reconciled people, and preached peace, was vindicated by God. Death, as it was meted out by religious and political authorities, was no match for the life that Jesus led and that he offered. God's response to the cross, to the marking and execution of Jesus as a criminal, was resurrection: raising Jesus to new, eternal life. God's raising of Jesus flies in the face of human habit to try to secure peace through violent and punitive means. This mode of ensuring security works only if the dead stay dead. But Jesus lived again! The one whom the powers of this world tried to expel returned.

Catholic life must consider the whole of the Paschal Mystery: Christ's suffering and death as a criminal, his resurrection as one vindicated by God, and consequently as one who is revealed to have lived as God wills—and even to be God himself—with his ministry of healing, forgiveness, reconciliation, and peace. If Catholics do this accounting, they should be persuaded that the reality of the Paschal Mystery must manifest itself in this world, here and now. It is not simply something that happened to the one man, Jesus, in the distant past. Today, the Paschal Mystery repudiates the instruments of death with which we tend to surround ourselves, the instruments that promise peace and security through violently enforced social hierarchies. Catholic priest and theologian James Alison argues that the Paschal Mystery, especially the linchpin of the resurrection, should impel pursuit of "the project of installing life in a culture of death."[10]

Concretely, with respect to the crisis of mass incarceration, this means that Catholics should distance themselves from the prison industrial complex. Vincent Lloyd reminds us that we worship a convicted and executed criminal whom the powers of this world deemed expendable, or even in need of elimination.[11] If we believe that this convicted and executed criminal was also raised and vindicated by God, we should work to dismantle infrastructures of social death that replicate on the bodies of incarcerated persons a fate similar to what Jesus endured. In imitation of the one who raised Jesus (Rom 4:24), Catholics should work toward social health, a politics that would restore life to those who have undergone social death by being warehoused in prisons. Reflection on the Paschal Mystery can energize political thinking and action in the direction of restorative rather than retributive approaches to social disorder and dysfunction.

The Paschal Mystery is celebrated liturgically by Catholics every day in Mass. We gather for a common meal to offer a sacrifice of praise to God in thanksgiving for the life, death, and resurrection of Jesus. The Eucharist, if viewed rightly, enacts inclusive table fellowship that invites people to a new life and challenges Catholics to restore life to those who have undergone social death.

The Politics of Mercy

The politics of mercy as it applies to the crisis of mass incarceration focuses on the same three spiritual works of mercy as we did with the crisis of solidarity surrounding migration: **admonishing the sinner**, **forgiving offenses**, and **bearing wrongs patiently**. The spiritual works of mercy pertain primarily to the need for reconciliation with God; the way that criminal justice in the United States tends to be pursued is a great offense against divine justice, which is always accompanied by God's mercy. As with the crisis surrounding migration, with regard to mass incarceration, dramatic conversion proves necessary. To these spiritual works we add the one corporal work of mercy of **visiting the prisoner**, which is also known as **ransoming the captive**. Ransoming the captive in the United States of the twenty-first century demands learning about the racial history behind mass incarceration, taking direct action to address the needs of communities torn apart by mass incarceration, visiting those in prison, and supporting antiracist efforts to transform society away from retributive and toward restorative order, away from a throwaway culture that attempts to dispose of people in prisons and toward a merciful order that fosters resurrected life in those who were socially dead.

Spiritual Works of Mercy: Restored Life

In Chapter 2 we introduced Keenan's grouping of the works of mercy of admonishing the sinner, forgiving offenses, and bearing wrongs patiently as the spiritual works of mercy that develop a habit of seeking reconciliation with God. These spiritual works fit naturally with the crisis of mass incarceration, where the extreme measures brought about by the retributive model for justice have led to an intolerable social situation. Lloyd calls mass incarceration an "abomination," and one has to agree.[12] These spiritual works challenge society as a whole to find a way to address the sins that break community without letting go of the life of forgiveness to which Jesus Christ calls everyone, and without relinquishing the virtue of patience, which helps us bear with one another through difficulty. There are obvious difficulties with all of these: mercy and forgiveness cannot mean allowing sin to go unopposed, and many harms (the sex abuse crisis in the Catholic Church provides a prime example) ought not be borne with patience, but rather met with vigorous rejection. How, then, can we think about and practice these spiritual works of mercy as part of a politics of mercy that aims to overturn mass incarceration?

In keeping with our theological analyses in this chapter, we could redesignate these spiritual works as fostering restored life after the death inflicted by sin (individual or structural) and harm (interpersonal or social). The Paschal Mystery of Jesus Christ must be a constant and consistent guide for spiritual practice. One could meditate, for instance, on how the cross of Christ reveals the seriousness of sin, and the burial of the dead Christ shows sin's depths. There is perhaps no firmer admonishment for sin than the recognition that Christ, dead on the cross, who perished because of the world's sin (Jn 1:29), was an innocent man (Lk 23:47). Human sin has dire consequences; we must not compound it by throwing lives (sometimes innocent ones) away. One could likewise reflect on the gravity of the Risen Christ's declaration to his disciples, "Whose sins you forgive are forgiven them, and whose sins you retain are retained" (Jn 20:23). While this quote is often taken by official Catholic theology as establishing the sacrament of penance, it has an even deeper meaning that should affect the spirituality of all Catholics. Being tasked with forgiving people, and knowing the danger of not doing so—potentially excluding people from Christ's forgiveness—precludes Catholics from being vengeful. The stakes are too high for us to support a vengeful system like mass incarceration. And one could contemplate further the significance of Christ bearing sins and insults (see, e.g., 1 Pet 1:24) for what it means to bear wrongs patiently, in such a way that it does not mean inaction or capitulation before injustice. Christ patiently bears the burden of our sins so as to lift the burden and pain of sin from those who fall victim to it. Such contemplation can foster a spirituality that coordinates with restorative justice, which supports victims harmed by crime and the families and communities to which they belong, and advocates giving them the attention and care that they need.

In 1999, the United States Conference of Catholic Bishops released an appeal on Good Friday for the abolition of the death penalty.[13] This appeal centered on the Paschal Mystery of Jesus Christ, who, we note again, was executed as a criminal. Meditation on the Paschal Mystery and what it means to admonish sinners, forgive offenses, and bear wrongs patiently must pass through this awareness that our savior was executed. This execution was an expression of human sin, not an act of justice. The Bishops remark that Christians must prayerfully witness against the death penalty, since this mode of punishment deforms community. They write:

> We oppose capital punishment not just for what it does to those guilty of horrible crimes but for what it does to all of us as a society. Increasing reliance on the death penalty diminishes all of us and is a sign of growing disrespect for human life. We cannot overcome crime by simply executing criminals, nor can we restore the lives of the innocent by ending the lives of those convicted of their murders. The death penalty offers the tragic illusion that we can defend life by taking life.

In opposition to such an illusion, and out of the font of a Christian spirituality of restored life, the bishops appeal for the abolition of the death penalty. Two decades after that statement, the United States—including, distressingly, a preponderance of American Catholics—has not heeded this call. Even so, in the face of the crisis of mass incarceration, this appeal must be expanded, on the grounds of a spirituality centered on the Paschal Mystery: not only the death penalty, but the prison industrial complex that is completely continuous with it in scope and in its spirit of vengeance and exclusion, must be reimagined. The Catholic Mobilizing Network, an organization dedicated to abolishing the death penalty and reforming the criminal justice system from a punitive to a restorative model of justice, does not go so far as to advocate abolishing the prison industrial complex.[14] Its efforts, however, if successful, would drastically reshape criminal justice as we know it, and, with hope, dismantle mass incarceration. The first step toward such a sweeping change, according to the politics of mercy we recommend, would be a spirituality of restored life, rendered concrete by proper recognition of sin's seriousness, of Christ's command to forgive, and of the need to support those burdened by the consequences of crime. The next step would be charitable action toward prisoners.

Charity: Visit the Prisoner

Visiting the prisoner and ransoming the captive emerge as central practices of mercy in response to the persecution and imprisonment of the earliest Christians. Jesus himself was a prisoner and was executed as a criminal, as we have already discussed. His earliest followers spent a great deal of time in prison, as the Acts of the Apostles and Paul's letters amply attest (Acts 5, 12, 16; 2 Cor 6:5, 11:23; Col 4:10; Eph 4:1; 2 Tim 1:16–18, 4:16–18). The God of Israel is praised numerous times in the scriptures for setting captives free (paradigmatically throughout Exodus, but also in Ps 69:33, 79:11, 102:20, 142:7, 146:7; and Is 42:6–7, 49:9, 61:1). Giving comfort and consolation to prisoners became a practice of mercy and encouragement for persecuted Christians. And ransoming or liberating the captive became a central imperative of Christian ministry in the early church. Later, when Christians were no longer imprisoned for their beliefs, the emphasis was placed on attending to the spiritual needs of the imprisoned and the demand that those placed in debtors' prison be freed. The Christian concern with the criminalization of poverty relates to the project of mass incarceration, which criminalizes poverty and then imposes what often amounts to a lifetime of debt on the imprisoned through fines, fees, interest, and restitution.

A wide array of individual and local initiatives exists to respond to the structural sin of mass incarceration. At the outset, it is important to recognize that mass incarceration represents a highly racialized system of social exclusion. It is easy to miss this fact, for two reasons. First, the new Jim Crow differs markedly from Jim Crow segregationist racism during the post–Civil War era (1865–1965) because the new Jim Crow's racialized mechanisms of exclusion are hidden from public view. Prisons are set apart from society and rarely seen by anyone other than the incarcerated, their relatives, and those who work in the prison industry. Most people are simply unaware that the expansion of prisons and the number of those incarcerated has proceeded at an alarming pace over the past forty years and that those most affected by this increase are from communities of color. Second, the project of mass incarceration has been sold to the public as a colorblind attempt to make society safe for law-abiding citizens. People commonly assume that persons who are incarcerated have committed a crime and deserve punishment—race, evidently, need not be a consideration. Therefore, the state and politicians can wash their hands of the racialized character of the U.S. criminal justice and prison systems.

The works of mercy aim to alleviate the suffering and social isolation of those marginalized within a social order, and so the act of visiting the incarcerated continues to represent a central practice of mercy in an era of mass incarceration. During his visit to the United States, Pope Francis visited prisoners in Philadelphia and made the following argument:

> All of us need to be cleansed, to be washed. All of us are being sought out by the Teacher, who wants to help us resume our journey. The Lord goes in search of us; to all of us he stretches out a helping hand. It is painful when we see prison systems which are not concerned to care for wounds, to soothe pain, to offer new possibilities. It is painful when we see people who think that only others need to be cleansed, purified, and do not recognize that their weariness, pain and wounds are also the weariness, pain and wounds of society. The Lord tells us this clearly with a sign: he washes our feet so we can come back to the table. The table from which he wishes no one to be excluded. The table which is spread for all and to which all of us are invited.[15]

Francis has made it a regular practice to visit prisons on Holy Thursday and to wash the feet of prisoners. This practice is an extension of the inclusive table fellowship Christ performed at the Last Supper (John 13:1–15). How might we practice this type of inclusive table fellowship in our own lives? A central practice in the Catholic tradition is prison ministry, which attempts to break with the logic of social death imposed on prisoners by carceral structures in the United States. Not only does the work of organizations like Catholic Prison Ministries Coalition (which promotes ministry to all people affected by incarceration) and Dismas Ministry (a national Catholic outreach for prisoners and others affected by crime) attend to the spiritual and social needs of the incarcerated.[16] Their work also provides those who engage in this ministry the opportunity to encounter God among those, like Christ himself, labelled criminals by the dominant social order and subjected to physical and social death.

Justice: Ransom the Captive

Catholic teaching and theology call Catholics to strive for the seemingly impossible and to labor to realize a social order rooted in mercy, inclusion, and restoration rather than punishment, exclusion, and social death. From a Catholic point of view, such political will should come from an application of the work of mercy of ransoming the captive and the theological reality of restoration achieved in Christ. Jesus Christ died as a "ransom for many" (Mk 10:45; Mt 20:28), having led a life of service to *all* his fellow persons. A politics of mercy arises from reflection on this Christological reality and its implications for society: to ransom the captive means to cooperate with the saving work of Christ, seeking to restore persons and entire social orders from the pathological drive toward punishment and exclusion.

In an extraordinary speech given to inmates in a prison in Ciudad Juárez, Mexico, in 2016, Francis offered a broad outline of a Catholic approach to prisons:

> Divine Mercy reminds us that prisons are an indication of the kind of society we are. In many cases they are a sign of the silence and omissions which have led to a throwaway culture, a symptom of a culture that has stopped supporting life, of a society that has abandoned its children. Mercy reminds

us that reintegration does not begin here within these walls; rather it begins before, it begins "outside," in the streets of the city. Reintegration or rehabilitation begins by creating a system which we could call social health, that is, a society which seeks not to cause sickness, polluting relationships in neighborhoods, schools, town squares, the streets, homes and in the whole of the social spectrum. A system of social health that endeavors to promote a culture which acts and seeks to prevent those situations and pathways that end in damaging and impairing the social fabric … The problem of security is not resolved only by incarcerating; rather, it calls us to intervene by confronting the structural and cultural causes of insecurity that impact the entire social framework. Jesus' concern for the care of the hungry, the thirsty, the homeless and prisoners sought to express the core of the Father's mercy. This becomes a moral imperative for the whole of society that wishes to maintain the necessary conditions for a better common life. It is within a society's capacity to include the poor, infirm and imprisoned, that we see its ability to heal their wounds and make them builders of a peaceful coexistence. Social reintegration begins by making sure that all of our children go to school and that their families obtain dignified work by creating public spaces for leisure and recreation, and by fostering civic participation, health services and access to basic services, to name just a few possible measures. The whole rehabilitation process starts here.[17]

In this passage Francis makes three important points that are relevant to a Catholic politics of mercy. First, he condemns prisons as a symptom of a **throwaway culture** that no longer values life and instead manages social problems through expulsion from the social order. Second, he argues that a Catholic commitment to mercy demands that we resist the tendency to deal with social insecurity and disorder primarily through processes of punishment. Francis offers here the broad outlines of an approach that reimagines prisons along preventative and restorative rather than punitive and retributive lines. The fundamental task is to create a system of social health that seeks to build "a culture which acts and seeks to prevent those situations and pathways that end in damaging and impairing the social fabric." The data about incarceration point to the fact that over 50% of those incarcerated suffer from mental disorders.[18] Because those incarcerated often come from poor and marginalized communities, this would necessitate increased spending on poverty prevention, education, and mental health services. Alarmingly, the data suggest that spending on prisons has grown at three times the rate of spending on education over the past thirty years.[19] Furthermore, an approach that seeks restoration must provide those incarcerated with paths of reentry that enable them to contribute to society. The forms of exclusion that felons face after they have served their sentences—lack of access to public assistance, housing benefits, the right to vote—should be abolished so as to provide social support for reintegration.

For Francis, we must ensure that mercy is made structural by working so that "the entire social framework" is rooted in Jesus's concern with "care of the hungry, the thirsty, the homeless and prisoners." This, and not retribution, is the merciful approach to dealing with social problems within society. But a third element should be added to Francis's vision in the American context. In view of the highly racialized character of the criminal justice system in the United States, ransoming the captive must entail explicitly antiracist initiatives and policies. Because mass incarceration emerged as a result of strategic and structural racism, its remedy must involve political and policy transformations that seek not only to eliminate the institutions that sustain the project of mass incarceration, but also offer creative responses to the types of structural inequalities that lead to criminal behavior.

In November 2019, Francis spoke to a group of prison ministers. He concluded his remarks with two images: windows and horizons.[20] Francis told them, "You cannot talk about paying a debt to society from a jail cell without windows." He continued: "There is no humane punishment without a horizon. No one can change their life if they don't see a horizon. And so many times we are used to blocking the view of our inmates." Windows and horizons are images of hope. The window signifies hope in the present for inmates currently in jails, prisons, and detention centers, that one day they will be able to live in the world outside. Horizons indicate hope for the future, that people released from prison will be able to enter a society that will welcome them back. Francis encourages those involved in pastoral care for prisoners to bring these images of windows and horizons to inmates. As for the rest of us, we should use the images of windows and horizons to envision a world without mass incarceration. The vast carceral apparatus we have, which includes not only jails, prisons, and detention centers, but also a wide-ranging and expanding surveillance system, is geared toward almost comprehensive social control. Its design includes almost no windows, virtually no ways to see past the prison industrial complex. Similarly, given its comprehensiveness, it is difficult to imagine a long-term societal goal, or horizon, beyond the prison industrial complex. But images can allow us to poke holes in this comprehensive, punitive system and the throwaway culture that sustains it. The images of windows and horizons permit us to imagine restorative justice—not just as an idea, but as a comprehensive expression of ransoming the captive, enlivened by a merciful culture.

Conclusion: Homeboy Industries

The story of Homeboy Industries, a gang intervention, rehabilitation, and reentry program in Los Angeles, California, can help us to concretize what the politics of mercy applied to mass incarceration might look like. In short, it would include a comprehensive implementation of restorative justice, not just as a response to discrete crimes, but as a way to build community—or as Homeboy Industries puts it, communities of **kinship** rooted in restored life after social death.

Los Angeles in the 1980s was the gang capital of the world. In keeping with the general trend toward mass incarceration and increased use of force in policing during that decade, such measures were implemented to try to stave off the tide of gang activity. These were thought to be proportionate with gang activity, which was often extremely violent, including burglaries, robberies, sale and abuse of drugs, assaults, drive-by shootings, manslaughter, and murder. In 1984, Jesuit priest Greg Boyle was appointed associate pastor of Dolores Mission parish in East Los Angeles, at that time the poorest parish in Los Angeles in an area with pronounced gang violence.[21] He became pastor in 1986. As he ministered to the people of his parish, including burying young people who had been killed by gang violence, Boyle and his parishioners began to explore possibilities for addressing the gang crisis in ways other than surveilling, arresting, and incarcerating gang members. At the forefront of this effort were parish leaders like Teresa Navarro and Paula Hernandez. They started by establishing an alternative school. They welcomed gang members to hang out on the parish grounds. Women from the parish walked to hot spots where shootings frequently occurred, where they prayed and sang to calm gang members primed for battle. They did these things because the people of this parish, along with their pastor, believed that this is what Jesus would do.

Such early efforts at Dolores Mission led to the 1988 founding of what would become Homeboy Industries. It began with a parish initiative called Jobs for the Future, which tried to get gang members jobs at nearby factories. When jobs did not materialize, the parish hired gang members to work in the community cleaning up graffiti, building a child care center, landscaping, and doing maintenance. This led to the opening of a bakery, then a tortilla stand in Grand Central Market, and in the summer of 1992, of Homeboy Industries as a multi-business venture that over the next decades would become the world's largest gang intervention, rehabilitation, and re-entry program.[22]

Today Homeboy Industries serves over 7,000 gang members per year, offering tattoo removal, mental health counseling, substance abuse support, education (e.g., GED tutoring), and job development (from basic skills like showing up to work on time to higher skills like solar panel installation). Remarkable though these services are—and more remarkable still that they are offered free of charge—the central aspect of Homeboy Industries is the focus placed on restored relationships and building communities of kinship. Trainees are given the opportunity to work with their enemies, members of rival gangs. Fr. Boyle emphasizes this continually: trainees should come to see their enemies as friends. When they do, they start to live out God's desire for all people, which Jesus expresses at the Last Supper: "that they may be one" (Jn 17:21). Just as Jesus lives in perfect kinship (family relationship) with God his Father, so may all people, if they learn to love their enemies (Mt 5:44; Lk 6:28), and to live in restored relationship with one another. Surely this is no easy task, sinners being sinners and the world being the way the world is. Fr. Boyle frequently points out that he has presided at more than 250 gang members' funerals. But he and all who work with him put their faith and hope in the God of mercy, who reconciles and restores even enemies to companionship.

Homeboy Industries illustrates well the politics of mercy, since it began with parish initiatives in prayer, worship, and charity. While retaining all of these dimensions, however, it has also grown in scale to serve a broad community in seeking an alternative, restorative model of justice to the punitive-retributive model that defines the U.S.

system of mass incarceration. Homeboy Industries' motto, printed on numerous items produced by its diverse businesses, is "Jobs Not Jails." And since 2014, with the establishment of the Global Homeboy Network, or a worldwide group of over 400 gang-intervention, rehabilitation, and re-entry programs, its influence is felt far and wide as a viable alternative to the prison industrial complex.

Fr. Boyle centers the work of Homeboy Industries on Jesus and his life of radical inclusion. We have reflected in this chapter on how the Paschal Mystery of Jesus should teach Catholics to question and to reject our human habits of exclusion, of trying to keep the peace through violence. It seems to us that Homeboy Industries answers in a powerful way the question "What becomes possible if you live as if the resurrection were real, as if the resurrection were really transforming our world today?" You could treat demonized people as dignified people. You could look at a criminal justice system built on strategies of racial suppression and mass incarceration and see the possibility of policies of education, job training, and, most important, kinship. To do what Homeboy Industries does is to believe in the Gospel, that it is real, that it means something now, that the Paschal Mystery can be lived.

Notes

1   Ina Jaffe, "Cases Show Disparity of California's Three Strikes Law," NPR, October 30, 2009, https://www.npr.org/templates/story/story.php?storyId=114301025.

2   Wilkerson's story is told in a number of different publications. See, for instance, Benjamin Moberg, "A Mandatory Mistake," *Sojourners*, February 19, 2015, https://sojo.net/articles/mandatory-mistake.

3   Jordan T. Camp, *Incarcerating the Crisis: Freedom Struggles and the Rise of the Neoliberal State* (Oakland: University of California Press, 2017), 3; and Michelle Alexander, *The New Jim Crow: Mass Incarceration in the Age of Colorblindness* (New York: The New Press, 2012), 60.

4   Ian Hanley Lopez, *Dog Whistle Politics: How Coded Racial Appeals Have Reinvented Racism & Wrecked the Middle Class* (New York: Oxford University Press, 2015).

5   Alexander, *The New Jim Crow*, 200.

6   Orlando Patterson, *Slavery and Social Death: A Comparative Study* (Cambridge, MA: Harvard University Press, 1982).

7   Joshua Price, *Prison and Social Death* (New Brunswick, NJ: Rutgers University Press, 2015).

8   Pope John Paul II, *Evangelium Vitae*, March 25, 1995, http://w2.vatican.va/ content/john-paul-ii/en/encyclicals/documents/hf_jp-ii_enc_25031995- evangelium-vitae.html.

9   United States Conference of Catholic Bishops, *Responsibility, Rehabilitation, and Restoration: A Catholic Perspective on Crime and Criminal Justice,* November 15, 2000, http://www.usccb.org/issues-and-action/human-life-and-dignity/ criminal-justice-restorative-justice/crime-and-criminal-justice.cfm#policy.

10   James Alison, *Raising Abel: The Recovery of the Eschatological Imagination* (New York: Crossroad Herder, 1996), 87–88.

11   Vincent Lloyd, "Prisons Are a Biblical Abomination," *Church Life Journal,* February 26, 2019, https://churchlifejournal.nd.edu/articles/prisons-are -a-biblical-abomination/.

12   Lloyd, "Prisons Are a Biblical Abomination."

13   United States Conference of Catholic Bishops, "A Good Friday Appeal to End the Death Penalty," April 2, 1999, http://www.usccb.org/issues-and-action/human- life-and-dignity/death-penalty-capital-punishment/good-friday-appeal.cfm.

14   For more information, see the website for the Catholic Mobilizing Network: https://catholicsmobilizing.org/.

15   Pope Francis, "Visit to Detainees at Curran-Fromhold Correctional Facility," http://w2.vatican.va/content/francesco/en/speeches/2015/september/ documents/papa-francesco_20150927_usa-detenuti.html.

16   For more information, see the websites for these organizations: Catholic Prison Ministries Coalition, https://www.catholicprisonministries.org/about-cpmc; and Dismas Ministry, https://dismasministry.org/.

17   Pope Francis, "Visit to the Penitentiary (Cereso N. 3) of Ciudad Juárez," https:// w2.vatican.va/content/francesco/en/speeches/2016/february/documents/ papa-francesco_20160217_messico-detenuti.html.

18   Olga Khazan, "Most Prisoners Are Mentally Ill," *The Atlantic*, April 7,
     2015, https://www.theatlantic.com/health/archive/2015/04/more-than
     -half-of-prisoners-are-mentally-ill/389682/.

19   Stephanie Kelly, "U.S. Spending on Prisons Grew at Three Times Rate of School
     Spending: Report," *Reuters*, July 27, 2016, https://www.reuters.com/article/
     us-usa-education-funding-idUSKCN0ZN2L2.

20   Cindy Wooden, "Pope Francis on Prison Systems: 'We will be judged on this,'"
     America, November 8, 2019, https://www.americamagazine.org/politics-
     society/2019/11/08/pope-francis-prison-systems-we-will-be-judged. For
     Francis's original remarks (in Italian, no English translation available), see Papa
     Francesco, "Discorso del Santo Padre Francesco ai Partecipanti all'Incontro
     Internazionale per i Resonsabili Regionali e Nazionali della Pastorale Carceraria,"
     November 8, 2019, http://w2.vatican.va/content/francesco/it/speeches/2019/
     november/documents/papa-francesco_20191108_pastorale-carceraria.html.

21   Fr. Boyle has told his story in numerous lectures, videos of which are readily
     accessible via the internet. He has also written two books that elaborate on the
     story: Gregory Boyle, *Tattoos on the Heart: The Power of Boundless Compassion*
     (New York: Simon & Schuster, 2010); and *Barking to the Choir: The Power of
     Radical Kinship* (New York: Simon & Schuster, 2017).

22   For more information see https://homeboyindustries.org/.

PART III

Violence

As with racism, people tend to think of violence primarily in terms of interpersonal acts of direct aggression, of terrorist attacks, or of warfare. But there are at least four forms of violence relevant to our discussion: direct, structural, slow, and cultural. Let us explain what each of these forms is, how each functions, and give a few examples of each.

- **Direct violence:** intentional acts of physical or verbal force directed at individuals or communities in order to inflict harm on them
    - Assault, rape, and murder
    - Terrorist attack
- **Structural violence:** ways in which violence is embedded in laws, institutions, policies, and broader social arrangements that harm individuals and communities on the basis of their gender, race, or economic status. As Paul Farmer argues, this form of violence is *structural* because it exists within political, economic, and social institutions and policies, and it is *violent* because it causes injury to persons.
    - The failure to provide access to basic goods to individuals and communities: food, shelter, health care.
- **Slow violence:** a form of violence that transpires at a slower temporal speed than direct violence. This term was coined by Rob Nixon in *Slow Violence and the Environmentalism of the Poor*

to signify the way in which the violence of climate change takes place over decades and even centuries but is no less lethal than more immediate threats.[1]

- The slowly drowning Island of Nauru in the South Pacific, whose inhabitants are the victims of the slow violence of the modern economic order and its climate catastrophes.

- **Cultural violence:** a symbolic or ideological way (or set of ways) of legitimating and authorizing violence. John Galtung argues that cultural violence makes direct, structural, and slow forms of violence seem permissible or even natural. It alters how we perceive a moral act from being "wrong" (red light) to "right" (green light), or at the very least "acceptable" (yellow light).[2]

  - **War:** It is viewed as necessary to spend $800 billion per year on defense and military spending, to sustain 800 military bases around the world, and to intervene periodically in foreign countries to protect the national security of the United States.

  - **Climate change:** denialism (the denial that there is a link between human activity and climate change) or arguments for deregulation of the economy (if we want economic growth, we need to remove laws that stand in the way of a fossil fuel–based economy).

There is one more important distinction to draw: between **visible** and **invisible** forms of violence. As the image on the next page demonstrates, our common-sense understanding of violence is often limited to visible forms of violence (direct violence). But beneath the surface, every society participates in invisible forms of violence (cultural, slow, and structural).

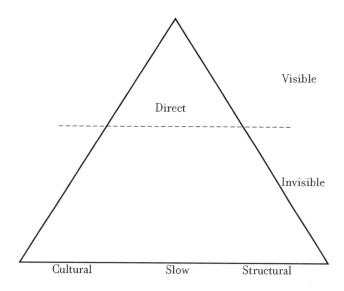

Figure III.1: Four forms of violence and their visibility or invisibility

Violence, then, is more than its manifestation through direct, overt, or fast forms that are immediately perceptible and clearly intentional. Furthermore, as with the four forms of racism, these forms of violence interrelate in complex ways. For instance, cultural violence is always operative in justifying and legitimating direct, structural, and slow forms of violence by making these other forms of violence seem permissible, rational, or even necessary.

The Catholic Church's history with respect to violence is, for certain, checkered. It is well known that the church freely participated in wars, colonialism, the slave trade, and numerous other atrocities. Likewise, Catholic teaching on violence is complicated, as we shall see. But the overriding commitment in recent official church teaching is to the peace of Christ. We find Catholic social teaching condemning the violence of nuclear war (John XXIII's *Pacem in Terris*, 1963), unnecessary war (the National Conference of Catholic Bishops' *The Challenge of Peace*, 1983), climate change (Francis's *Laudato Si'*, 2015), and sexual violence (the United States Conference of Catholic Bishops' *When I Call for Help*, 1992/2002). These recent writings give hope that, at least in its official capacity, the church is reflecting more determinedly of late about how to let the light of Christ's peace shine in the world.

This part of the book aims to contribute to this effort by reimagining the works of mercy in light of contemporary crises of violence. Just as the works of mercy are not traditionally set explicitly against racism, they neither tend to be seen as an explicit program for fostering peace. But given crises like militarism and environmental destruction, it is incumbent on us to reimagine the works of mercy in view of these structures of sin and the violent cultures that support them, lest the Catholic Church be complicit with them and silent about them. We stand convinced that the reimagined works of mercy could function as a framework for building a **just peace**. The latter phrase, which clearly combines concerns for justice and peace, has become the goal for Catholic social thought and practice. To bury the dead and visit the sick in our world today must mean expressly supporting just peace, which involves demanding that the military-industrial complex be scaled back and resources diverted into community building, poverty reduction, education, and other initiatives aimed at restoring social order; and working toward economies, polities, and societies that are not dependent on fossil fuels and constant production of waste. Catholics must advocate a politics that squares more nearly with the peace Christ gives and with the healing of creation that his Incarnation (God coming in human flesh) effects. Thankfully, there are Catholic organizations like Catholic Relief Services and Bethlehem Farm that are doing just this.

Notes

1   Rob Nixon, *Slow Violence and the Environmentalism of the Poor* (Cambridge, MA: Harvard University Press, 2011).

2   John Galtung, "Cultural Violence," *Journal of Peace Research* 27, no. 3 (August 1990): 291–305.

CHAPTER 4

War

Introduction

NEARLY 3,000 PEOPLE WERE brutally murdered in New York City on September 11, 2001. The response of the United States of America was to declare a "War on Terror" that has become an endless war in central Asia and the Middle East and has led to the deaths of at least 801,000 more people. Of those killed, it is estimated that 335,000 were civilians.[1] These numbers do not account for indirect death, that is, death from displacement, disease, and lack of access to basic resources. Analysts estimate that if indirect violence were accounted for, the number killed would be more than 1 million.[2] Furthermore, 21 million people have been displaced as a result of U.S. military campaigns in Afghanistan, Iraq, Syria, and Pakistan, often encountering the lack of compassion for migrants that we discussed in Chapter 2. Independent of the debate concerning whether the wars in Afghanistan and Iraq constitute a legitimate response to the attack on the United States on 9/11, these raw numbers provide a sobering contrast between the events of that day and the results of the War on Terror.

Young people reading this book were likely born after 9/11 and have never known a time when the United States was not at war. Unfortunately, this reality does not represent a significant departure from U.S. foreign policy after World War II, insofar as the country has been involved without interruption in some form or another in conflicts around the world.[3] In a sense, therefore, it is not an overstatement to observe that U.S. foreign policy is predicated on **endless**

war and therefore endless sacrifice. The death toll resulting from the interventions in the Middle East is one example of this sacrifice. The Vietnam War is another, which resulted in the deaths of not only 58,272 American soldiers, but also well over one million Vietnamese soldiers and Vietnamese, Cambodian, and Laotian civilians. These numbers concretely signify the unnecessary sacrifices of war, which involve the brutal destruction of people, materials, funds, cultural cohesion, and health. What is important is that these sacrifices are unnecessary. The violence of war represents one means of attempting to resolve social conflict. But other means exist and, as we argue in this chapter, they are means that are more consistent with the peace of Christ.

Before we examine war, we should note the symmetry between the current chapter on war and the previous chapter on mass incarceration. Both mass incarceration and militarism serve as social systems that utilize violence in order to deal with those deemed threatening to the social order: criminals (incarceration) and foreign threats, or, more recently, "terrorists" (militarism). Both have built up massive structures to pursue these violent processes: the prison-industrial complex and the military-industrial complex. In both cases, we argue that a Catholic response to threats (perceived or real) should involve (1) a critique of the appropriateness of the prison- or military-industrial complexes as structures for dealing with social problems, and (2) support for a preventative (social spending/development) and restorative (reconciliation) approach as a more properly Catholic response to social problems.

Crisis

War represents a politics of sacrifice in which the destruction of soldiers, foreign combatants, and innocent bystanders is viewed as necessary to preserve security. While the entirety of U.S. history is replete with examples of foreign interventionism, since World War II the examples have become more abundant. During the postwar period, the United States built a national security state that has sustained an expansive military footprint around the world, with the chief aim of resisting communism. This postwar national security state apparatus still exists, even after the fall of Soviet Communism in 1989. It consists of:

- **Military bases:** Over 800 U.S. military bases in 80 countries, a figure that exceeds the total number of foreign military bases of all other countries combined (Russia is the closest to the United States, with a possible 40 bases in nine foreign countries).[4]
- **Military spending:** If we combine funding for the Department of Defense, Homeland Security, the State Department, and the FBI, the estimate is that for the 2019–2020 fiscal year the United States will devote almost $900 billion to military spending.[5] The country spends more on national defense than the next seven countries combined (China, Saudi Arabia, India, France, Russia, the United Kingdom, and Germany). China, at approximately $164 billion in 2019, spends the second most (and the population of China is four times that of the United States).[6]
- **Military personnel:** Over 1.3 million active-duty military and over 800,000 reserve members. Further, the United States has approximately 20 million veterans.
- **Military-industrial complex:** In 1961, President Dwight D. Eisenhower (a former Army General) warned of the creation of a "military-industrial complex" that would bring together the interests of military officials and the defense industry to expand military spending in the United States. Critics argue that defense contractors advocate for expansion in order to profit from military spending, and military officials support this expansion to enhance their capacity to defend U.S. interests around the world.

The construction of this vast network of national security agencies, businesses, and personnel has supported the country's engagement in what critics describe as the "endless war" that followed the end of World War II. The creation of the military-industrial complex during the Cold War allowed the United States to be involved in military conflicts around the world during the Cold War itself (1945–1989) and now the War on Terror (2001–). During the Cold War, the United States engaged in overt and covert military operations that resulted in the overthrow of democratically elected presidents in Guatemala, Iran, Chile, Nicaragua, and the Congo, "total wars" in Korea and Vietnam, and various proxy wars during civil wars in El Salvador, Honduras, and Nicaragua.[7] In the immediate aftermath of the end of the Cold War in the 1990s, the country continued its military operations with the first Iraq War (Operation Desert Storm), interventions in Bosnia and Serbia, and operations in a dozen other countries. With the attack on September 11, 2001, the United States entered another stage of conflict with the War on Terror, which has led to military interventions or wars in Afghanistan, Iraq, Libya, and Syria. Remarkably, since the end of the Cold War (1989), the United States has used military force over 200 times (including in Somalia, Yemen, Colombia, Haiti, Liberia, and the Philippines).[7]

The U.S. foreign policy establishment has promoted military interventions as wars of necessity in which the country had little choice but to engage in armed conflict to defend the security of U.S. citizens. In reality, virtually every U.S. intervention after World War II has been a war of choice. Why has the United States so frequently conflated wars of necessity with wars of choice? There are compli- cated reasons for this tendency, but an important factor is the dis- course of **American exceptionalism**, a form of cultural violence that claims that when the country uses force, it is always and inevitably morally justified. A number of symbolic markers have been utilized to convey this sense of uniqueness. They range from characterizing the United States in biblical terms as the "New Israel" (based loosely on a variety of texts in the biblical Book of Revelation), or a people chosen by God, to the colonialist ideology of Manifest Destiny that legitimated westward expansion across the North American conti- nent. We now commonly talk in terms of American exceptionalism and the view that the United States is a unique nation in world history in terms of its moral probity and its political mission for the world. This belief in exceptionalism is shared by Americans on the politi- cal left and the political right and employed to justify the use of mili- tary force abroad. Madeline Albright, the Secretary of Defense in the Clinton administration, succinctly summarized this position: "If we have to use force, it is because we are America; we are the indispens- able nation. We stand tall and we see further than other countries into the future."[8] According to this ideological framework, everything that the United States does is justified (tragedies of past) and authorized (future interventions) because it possesses a unique moral standing among nations and has a distinctive mission for the world. This pre- sumed innocence blinds the country to the actual motivations that drive its foreign policy, obscuring the violence it often perpetrates in the name of freedom and democracy.

As with mass incarceration, the American public often experiences a forced apathy with respect to the project of endless war. Both mass incarceration and endless war have generated institutional networks (the prison-industrial complex and the military-industrial complex) that have taken on an air of necessity and permanence. This sense of permanence is predicated on the hiddenness of the sacrifices performed by these systems. For example, it is rare that we know of the cost of these systems in concrete or personalist terms, because these systems turn people into statistics, making them faceless and nameless. It is uncommon that we know the cost of the sacrifices of war except perhaps in terms of the loss of lives among *American* soldiers—those we regard as "our own," which is to say nothing of people, lands, and biospheres abroad.

Catholic Social Thought

Catholic social thought on peace is rooted in the peace of Christ, which Jesus himself designates as the "peace that the world does not give" (Jn 14:27). It is certainly the case that Jesus's life is defined by his desire to enact a politics of inclusive justice for the marginalized and oppressed, but of equal importance is his commitment to peace. This can be observed in a few of Jesus's teachings to his disciples in the Gospels:

- "Blessed are they who hunger and thirst for righteousness, for they will be satisfied. Blessed are the merciful, for they will be shown mercy. Blessed are the clean of heart, for they will see God. *Blessed are the peacemakers, for they will be called children of God*" (Mt 5:6–9, emphasis added).[9]
- "You have heard that it was said, 'An eye for an eye and a tooth for a tooth.' But I say to you, offer no resistance to one who is evil. When someone strikes you on your right cheek, turn the other cheek and offer it to him as well" (Mt 5:39).
- "You have heard that it was said, 'You shall love your neighbor and hate your enemy.' But I say to you, love your enemies, and pray for those who persecute you" (Mt 5:43). Paul says, in a

similar vein, "If your enemy is hungry, feed him; if he is thirsty, give him something to drink" (Rom 12:20, quoting Prv 25:21).

- "Put your sword back into its sheath, for all who take the sword will perish by the sword" (Mt 26:52).

The Catholic tradition has made its own the centrality of peace to Jesus's life and teaching. The Catholic Mass, for instance, includes an expression of peace at its very center, just prior to the reception of communion. So, too, does peace have pride of place in Catholic social thought. But the implications of Jesus's teachings on peace entail complex and challenging questions: What is peace (is it merely the absence of direct violence)? How is peace best realized? What types of actions are permitted to bring about peace? A number of different Catholic approaches to war result from the complexities that arise from a Catholic commitment to peace: pacifism, just war, and peacebuilding.[9]

The early church was **pacifist**. It took Jesus's teaching literally and viewed the use of violence as inconsistent with the demands of discipleship. Christian pacifists up to and including today contend that it is morally improper to bear arms, to support or participate in violent action under any circumstances, and that a nonviolent approach to social conflict was endorsed by Jesus himself. While the just war tradition dominated official Catholic teaching on conflict from the time of St. Augustine (354–430) to the nineteenth century, in the twentieth century we witnessed a reinvigoration of the pacifist tradition. From individuals (Dorothy Day and Daniel Berrigan) and communal witness (Catholic Worker and Pax Christi) to official Catholic teaching (John XXIII, with *Pacem in Terris*, and Vatican II, specifically *Gaudium et Spes*), we have witnessed a reaffirmation of pacifism as an enduring Catholic way of witnessing to Christ's peace.

While the early church was pacifist and pacifism remains a radical expression of Catholic discipleship, the Catholic tradition came to justify the use of violence under very specific circumstances in order to defend the lives of the innocent and to protect the common good. The **just war** tradition codifies four criteria that must be fulfilled for Catholics to support or to participate in warfare. The tradition's four criteria serve as a moral framework for assessing when it is legitimate to use violence in defense of peace. The *Catechism of the Catholic Church* describes these four criteria in the following way:

- **Self-defense:** War must be the response to prior aggression. The damage inflicted by the aggressor on the nation or community of nations must be lasting, grave, and certain.
- **Last resort:** All other means of putting an end to the aggression must have been shown to be impractical or ineffective.
- **Probability of success:** There must be serious prospects for success.
- **Proportional response:** The use of arms must not produce evils and disorders graver than the evil to be eliminated. The power of modern means of destruction (e.g., nuclear weapons) weighs very heavily in evaluating this condition (*CC*, 2309).

Because these function as broad criteria, interpretations vary regarding what just war criteria warrant when applied to specific conflicts. **Just war realism** posits that because evil exists in the world, and since this evil is manifest in the attempt by aggressors to inflict violence on the innocent, it is necessary under specific circumstances for nation-states to protect their citizens with military force.[10] Others argue that the just war tradition serves as a framework for moral discernment that should be used to limit war and to criticize authorities that enter into conflict without utilizing just war criteria as a moral framework for discernment. Proponents of this position, often referred to as **just war pacifism**, argue that just war principles virtually rule out the moral legitimacy of contemporary warfare.[11]

Although the common-sense position of most U.S. Catholics is likely more closely aligned with the just war realist position, the tradition of Catholic social teaching has moved increasingly away from just war principles and their legitimation of warfare. From John XXIII to Francis, Catholic popes have focused their reflections on the development of a politics of peace.

In 1963, John XXIII published *Pacem in Terris* (*PT*) in response to the nuclear arms race. He argued that "disputes which may arise between nations must be resolved by negotiation and agreement, and not by recourse to arms" and that "it no longer makes sense to maintain that war is a fit instrument with which to repair the violation of justice" (*PT*, 127). In his 1967 encyclical on economic development, *Populorum Progressio* (*PP*), Paul VI argued that "development is the new name for peace" (*PP*, 76). He added the following year, in his message for the first World Day of Peace, "Peace is the only true direction of human progress—and not the tensions caused by ambitious nationalisms, nor conquests by violence, nor repressions which serve as mainstay for a false civil order."[12] And in a speech given in 1972, he contended, "If you want peace, work for justice" (a reflection on Isaiah 32:17 and a direct rebuttal of the Latin adage that "if you want peace, prepare for war").[13]

During his papacy, John Paul II pointed to nonviolent witness as the key element that brought down the Soviet Union. He contrasted this with the militaristic buildup during the Cold War, which was heightened by Ronald Reagan. He critiqued the 1991 Gulf War, condemned the 2003 Iraq War, and expressed concern about the effect on innocent bystanders of the United States' invasion of Afghanistan in 2001. With John Paul II, Benedict XVI (at the time, Joseph Cardinal Ratzinger) rejected the rationale for the Iraq War and questioned whether it is possible to enact a just war in the twenty-first century: "There were not sufficient reasons to unleash a war against Iraq. To say nothing of the fact that, given the new weapons that make possible, or perhaps even necessitate, destruction that includes noncombatants, today we should be asking ourselves if it is still licit to admit the very existence of a 'just war.'"[14]

In "Nonviolence: A Style of Politics for Peace," his message celebrating the fiftieth anniversary of the World Day of Peace, Francis offers the following observation: "Violence is not the cure for our broken world. Countering violence with violence leads at best to forced migrations and enormous suffering, because vast amounts of resources are diverted to military ends and away from the everyday needs of young people, families experiencing hardship, the elderly, the infirm and the great majority of people in our world."[15] Francis calls for peacebuilding through "active and creative nonviolence" as "the natural and necessary complement to the Church's continuing efforts to limit the use of force by the application of moral norms" (an oblique reference to the just war tradition).[16]

Official Catholic teaching is not a pacifist tradition. It maintains that under very rare circumstances, when all other means of resolving a conflict have been exhausted, the use of force can serve as a legitimate form of self-defense against aggressors. Each pope from John XXIII to Francis has recognized that under certain circumstances it might be necessary to employ force as a form of self-defense or a support for humanitarian causes, but their message remains primarily focused on nonviolent approaches to conflict resolution. Remarkably, since Vatican II no pope has endorsed or approved of a specific act of war or military intervention.[17] The rest of this chapter adheres to this path, advocating **just peace** rather than just war as the most suitable Catholic response to social conflict.

Where just war focuses on procedures for discerning under what conditions it is moral to use force, just peace focuses on how to create a more enduring peace by resolving conflicts through peaceful means and preventing conflicts from taking place by eliminating their root causes. In particular, just peace supports nonviolent direct action, conflict resolution, just and sustainable economic development, and grassroots peacebuilding as a means of building a more reconciled world.

The Politics of Mercy

The politics of mercy as it applies to the crisis of endless war focuses on the spiritual work of mercy of **praying for the dead** and the corporal work of mercy of **burying the dead**. The spiritual work of praying for the dead fosters a spirituality of reconciliation between enemies and of building communities so capacious that they extend even beyond this present life. Such a spirituality contrasts sharply with war's production of death, insistence upon conflict between enemies, and violent imposition and policing of borders. Burying the dead in the face of twenty-first-century U.S. militarism means even more than (while still including) giving dignified burials to deceased human persons. It challenges Christians to mourn the deaths of all human persons and to hope for their resurrection; this stands in contrast to war, which makes sense only when people limit mourning to "our dead," and hope that "their dead" stay dead. Burying the dead also demands taking concrete action to raise the alarm about U.S. militarism's anti-life character, and, in some cases, adopting radical measures of nonviolent protest to stir imaginations to envision a world where there will always be conflicts, but there will never again be endless war. As with the politics of mercy that responds to mass incarceration, a politics of mercy responding to war should support efforts to transform society away from a punitive order and toward a restorative order; away from a throwaway culture that justifies disposing of people on battlefields and beyond, and toward a merciful order that fosters the peace of Christ through ever more equitable, just, and expansive communities—away from endless war and toward just peace.

Spiritual Work: Prayer for the Dead

As we have done with the other spiritual works of mercy, we draw inspiration from Keenan. He treats **praying for the living and the dead** as the seventh and final spiritual work of mercy.[18] We have already applied the other six spiritual works of mercy to the three crises of inequality, mass deportation, and mass incarceration. This seventh spiritual work of mercy will cover the last two crises—namely, war and the climate crisis—which we consider to be crises of violence. We divide this work into two: prayer for the dead and prayer for the living. A politics of mercy that addresses war begins with prayer for the dead, since war is defined by its production of death. A politics of mercy that addresses the climate crisis opens with prayer for the living, in the hope that life will be preserved from mass extinction and catastrophe.

Prayer that is practiced specifically as a spiritual work of mercy is a special type. Keenan calls it the prayer of **supplication**. It is the kind of prayer in which a person begs from God, argues, pleads, and even bargains with God. It is prayer that turns to God with a need. This kind of prayer has three dimensions: **effective**, **unitive**, and **transformative**. "Effective prayer" means that the supplication is specific and concrete; one tells God exactly what one wants. One does this even if the specific results one seeks seem impossible. "Unitive prayer" means that in one's supplication, with Christ's help, one draws near to those for whom one prays. Consequently, this dimension of prayer builds community. "Transformative prayer" means a few things. Like the other works of mercy, the spiritual work of prayer transforms the one who does it: "By entering into another's chaos we are affected and shaped both by our loved one and by Christ."[19] Concern for another, expressed in prayer, reshapes what one desires. The power of Christ enables one to confront one's fears, for oneself and others, with greater resolve. But most of all, fervent prayer fosters hope by occasioning an encounter with divine love.

These three dimensions of prayer can illuminate the Catholic spirituality that opposes war and environmental destruction and seeks to build a politics of mercy and a community of life. Here let's consider prayer for the dead as it addresses the crisis of endless war. Effective prayer for the dead pleads with God to fulfill the eschatological promise that "they shall beat their swords into plowshares and their spears into pruning hooks; One nation shall not raise the sword against another, nor shall they train for war again" (Is 2:4). This prayer begs God that the lives lost to war will not be in vain—that peace will finally arrive, not as a result of war but as a result of its ceasing. If effective prayer means asking for exactly what one wants, then this petition is exactly what must be begged of God. Unitive prayer for the dead ventures to do exactly what war and its supporting ideologies would prohibit: prayer for the dead among one's enemies, so that one may enter into communion with them. This prayer cries out to God for the strength to live Jesus's most difficult teachings, to love one's enemies—which he accompanies with the command to pray for those by whom one is persecuted, hated, cursed, and mistreated (Mt 5:44; Lk 6:27–28). Transformative prayer for the dead aligns perfectly with effective prayer, with one slight, further addition: it creates hope within the one practicing it not only that the dead have not died in vain, but also that they will rise with Christ, and that every "sovereignty, authority, and power" that relies on war will be destroyed (1 Cor 15:22–24). Transformative prayer for the dead should create a hope-filled space that sustains the resurrection-suffused way of life that we began discussing in Chapter 3.

We should point out the close coordination between the corporal work of burying the dead and the spiritual work of praying for the dead. Both works have as their theological foundation the dignity of the human person, which we have returned to again and again. Just as people must be treated as dignified and called to grandeur and glorification during their lives, so should they be cared for in death. While it may seem remote from the battlefields of war, the **Mass of Christian Burial**, or the Catholic funeral rite, provides an interesting counterpart. The Mass of Christian Burial, which profoundly combines the corporal work of mercy of burying the dead and the spiritual work of praying for the dead, contrasts perfectly with the treatment of human bodies in war. Instead of exposing, attacking, maiming, and demeaning the human body, as happens in war, at the Mass of Christian Burial we witness a covering of the human body with a white cloth signifying Christ's protection from sin and death; a blessing with incense and holy water; a gathering of the person's life, both in body and story, before the altar; and a commending of the person's body and soul to God's mercy. Again, the contrast between violence and mercy could hardly be starker. While we should avoid any sort of liturgical ideal- ism that attempts to read social life directly off of Catholic sacramental practice, we would be equally remiss not to learn important lessons for a politics of mercy from the Mass of Christian Burial. It may not be a social program, but it is not as far from concrete efforts toward peace- building as one may think. And certainly it is a powerful expression of a Catholic spirituality of mercy.

Charity: Burying the Dead

What is the meaning of "bury the dead"? This corporal work of mercy is exactly what it sounds like, but also more, as we have just noted with our consideration of the Mass of Christian Burial. Christopher Allen- Douçot, co-founder of the Hartford Catholic Worker in Hartford, Connecticut, states that war is the opposite of the works of mercy: "War destroys homes, it burns crops, it poisons water, it denies health care. It doesn't bury the dead; it leaves the dead exposed on the battle- field."[20] We pursue this insight here as it informs charitable action that addresses the crisis of endless war.

The broader meaning of bury the dead is that people—*all* peo- ple, not just "our own"— must be treated with dignity even through death, and this is so because Catholics believe that life continues beyond death and, furthermore, community extends beyond death. Burying the dead as a corporal work of mercy relates closely to core Christian beliefs in **resurrection of the body** and **the communion of the saints**. Earlier we covered the idea and reality of resurrection in Chapter 3 when considering the Paschal Mystery of Jesus Christ. The communion of the saints is a further corollary of this. Belief in the communion of the saints means that all those who have lived in accordance with Christ's teachings and, even more importantly, have placed their faith and hope in God's forgiving mercy in Christ and God's gift of Godself in the Holy Spirit, lead new lives in heaven, yet they still relate to the living in our world through prayer and inter- cession (communication of the living's needs to Christ). In short, Christian community includes the living and the dead. This is why we practice the spiritual work of praying for the living and the dead in the first place. If death is the ultimate border, community transcends the ultimate border—as St. Paul asks, "Death, where is your sting?" (1 Cor 15:55). War violently enforces human-made borders; death is war's law. Core beliefs of Christianity call war into question. They demand practices that oppose it.

To address the crisis of endless war at the level of Christian charity is, consequently, to find direct ways to uphold the human dignity of the living and the dead in the spirit of resurrection, the communion of the saints, and the peace of Christ. Direct action to serve people in need in the midst of war is, of course, imperative.

We'll focus our attention, though, on protest as direct action, since protest contests the notion that Americans consent to the endless wars perpetrated in their name. Numerous Catholics participate each year in a variety of protests against war and war-making. The Hartford Catholic Worker community participates frequently in protests at the U.S. Naval Submarine Base New London in Groton, Connecticut. They have protested on the commissioning dates of new Virginia-class nuclear submarines, death-dealing vehicles that cost $2.7 billion apiece (a noteworthy fact in our era of inequality). While their protest actions are peaceful and, for the most part, silent, the Catholic Workers, by standing on a main highway near the entrance to the base, aim to raise an objection to U.S. militarism, to its addiction to violence, to its refusal of peaceful community, and to its squandering of resources. The hope is not that any single protest will turn the tide against U.S. militarism, but that these small efforts will multiply, by little and by little (as Dorothy Day used to say), into more protests, and eventually begin to foster a culture of mercy, peace, and dignified treatment of the living and the dead.

Protest as direct action largely concerns the **imagination**—not as fantasy, but as the capability for envisioning possibilities for the world. Many Catholic Workers and others have long engaged in the study of war, peace, community building, and the history of anti-war activism (Catholic and non-Catholic); they have debated, reflected, and prayed extensively on what they have learned. All this effort has been expended to develop a new imagination that can reach beyond our current reality to something new. By knowing well what we have, and seeing how it contrasts sharply with the Gospels and Catholic tradition, Catholic anti-war activists position themselves to point out that an alternative to endless war is possible and, on Catholic principles, necessary. One of the only ways that U.S. militarism survives so undisturbed and undeterred is that so few Catholics learn about the actuality of the U.S. war machine. Even fewer take the additional time to learn how Catholic teaching calls it into question, and fewer still allow these insights to affect their political and social imagination.

In an atmosphere marked by American exceptionalism, it is virtually impossible to imagine an alternative to endless war. It is difficult to disrupt and undermine the mythos surrounding U.S. militarism. Catholic life has, for the most part, been made to look indistinguishable from support for endless war, since U.S. Catholics tend to be formed as citizens first, with Catholicism being grafted onto this primary identity. Given this situation, we feel the need to examine radical anti-war movements as the opening steps toward Catholic alternatives to our militarist present.

Dorothy Day's civil disobedience in the 1950s is one such example. Day opposed civil defense drills, which she regarded as preparing the entire U.S. population for war.[21] On multiple occasions in the 1950s, she publicly refused to take cover during these drills—not to do so constituted a misdemeanor in New York State. Day was arrested on five separate occasions for such disobedience of the law, spending a total of six weeks in jail. She did this because she believed that civil disobedience made a vital Christian contribution. She reports in a 1957 piece on her incarceration:

> So many in these days have taken violent steps to gain the things of this world—war to achieve peace; coercion to achieve freedom; striving to gain what slips through the fingers. We might as well give up our great desires, at least our hopes of doing great things toward achieving them, right at the beginning. In a way it is the paradox of the Gospel, of giving up one's life in order to save it.
>
> That, in effect, is what we did when we went to jail. It was part of it. We were setting our faces against the world, against things as they are, the terrible injustice of our capitalist industrial system which lives by war and by preparing for war; setting our faces against race hatreds and all nationalist strivings…. We made our gesture; we disobeyed a law.[22]

Day acknowledges that her action constituted turning against the world; in this case "the world" included the vast majority of her fellow U.S. Catholics, who placidly took part in civil defense drills so as not to disrupt protocols or shirk what were presented as "patriotic duties." By sitting on a park bench during a mock, fictional nuclear "disaster," Day and her companions bore radical witness to the peace of Christ against a culture of warmaking. Such action should still stir the Catholic imagination.

A second example brings us up to the present day, though its roots stretch back forty years. Catholic activists involved in the **Plowshares Movement** have witnessed in dramatic fashion against the ever-present threat of nuclear war. This movement began in September 1980, when a group of eight peacekeepers, led by Catholic activists Daniel and Philip Berrigan, infiltrated General Electric Building #9 in King of Prussia, Pennsylvania, which manufactured parts used on nuclear missiles. The activists hammered on the nose cones of nuclear warheads and poured blood on war-planning documents. They caused relatively little damage but were rapidly jailed. They performed this action to symbolically disarm the U.S. nuclear arsenal and to enact in real life the prophecy of Isaiah that we have already quoted: "they shall beat their swords into plowshares" (Is 2:4). The Plowshares Eight served between five days and eighteen months in jail. Since their demonstration, over 100 Plowshares actions have taken place around the globe.

Among those who have participated are Catholic peace activists Paul Magno and Sister Megan Rice. Magno writes in an article commemorating the Plowshares Movement's thirty-fifth anniversary about their response to the most frequently asked question about Plowshares actions:

> Why this approach, which seems to cost so much and accomplish so little? We must begin somewhere, we answer. We are confronting an existential threat that calls everything into question—not simply the future of humanity or of the planet, as grave as that threat is, but a threat to who and what we are as human beings, and what we believe in. Plowshares actions simply try to state where authentic humanity needs to stand, *wants* to stand (if it finds freedom to do so): in opposition to nihilism. A readiness to wreck everything represents the worst of what people are capable of. Preparations for war are invariably conducted by the powerful and privileged in the service of

their own imagined entitlements, and at the expense of ordinary people who
have little influence over anything—the modern nuclear sword least of all.[23]

Plowshares actions may seem extreme, since they include trespassing
on military property, some destruction of property, and the eventual
arrest and imprisonment of the activists involved. But Magno's pointing to the symbolic character of these actions, and their opposition to
nihilism (belief in nothing—a grave violation of faith), suggests their
sacramental, faithful, and Catholic character.

In April 2018, a group of seven Plowshares activists, including Martha Hennessy, granddaughter of Dorothy Day, and Elizabeth
McAlister, wife of Philip Berrigan, undertook another Plowshares
action at the Kings Bay Naval Submarine Base in St. Mary's, Georgia,
which is the largest nuclear submarine base in the world. They acted
on the fiftieth anniversary of the assassination of Dr. Martin Luther
King, Jr., to highlight anew his opposition to the interconnected evils
of racism, militarism, and materialism. As their website puts it, "They
hoped to call attention to the ways in which nuclear weapons kill every
day, by their mere existence and maintenance."[24] By reading an indictment against the U.S. government for war crimes, hammering on rep-
licas of Trident nuclear missiles, spilling blood on the naval base's
seal, and spray painting exhortations to repentance at the base, these
Catholic peacemakers attempted to stir imaginations to envision a
world beyond preparation for nuclear war. In doing so, they practiced
Christian charity as part of a broader politics of mercy.

Justice: A Style of Politics for Peace

In Chapter 3, "Mass Incarceration," we examined Pope Francis's preventative and restorative approach to mass incarceration. We will now
apply the same framework to war. In modern Catholic social thought,
the stated aim is to abolish war and violence as the central means for
resolving social conflict. For instance, on World Peace Day in 1999,
John Paul II observed that

recent history clearly shows the failure of recourse to violence as a means
for resolving political and social problems. War destroys, it does not build
up; it weakens the moral foundations of society and creates further divisions

and long-lasting tensions. And yet the news continues to speak of wars and armed conflicts, and of their countless victims. How often have my Predecessors and I myself called for an end to these horrors! I shall continue to do so until it is understood that war is the failure of all true humanism.

Similarly, at a vigil prayer for peace in St. Peter's Square as the United States considered military action in Syria, Francis argued that "violence and war lead only to death, they speak of death! Violence and war are the language of death!" He suggested that an alternative must be sought. He joined with Paul VI in calling for the abolition of war and seeking a peace that is inseparable "from the demands of justice."[25]

Paul VI, John Paul II, Benedict, and Francis have all insisted that the most effective means of securing peace is not military intervention but nonviolent methods that seek justice. These popes, along with John XXIII, have attempted to foster "a style of politics for peace."[26] We have argued that this style of politics stems from a shift in focus from just war to just peace. Just peace offers a positive vision for realizing Christ's peace. It does so by focusing on the integral relationship that exists between justice and peace. More recent Catholic thinking and action has also come to emphasize the importance of reconciliation for fostering justice and peace.

A Catholic just peace approach is not critical of the existence of the U.S. military, but of its size, practices, and the amount of spending it devotes to maintaining its footprint around the world. A Catholic just peace raises related questions about why so little is spent on development and on efforts to support peacebuilding around the world. Cardinal Blase Cupich, the Archbishop of Chicago, has compellingly summarized this problem in his essay "Witnessing to a Consistent Ethic of Solidarity":

> The question is not whether there should be military spending, but what is the needed proportion so that other ways of making us safe, secure, and whole are not neglected. Our nation already spends more on its military than any other nation on earth. It has been estimated that the world spent about $1.6 trillion on military funding in 2015. U.S. military spending amounted to about 37 percent of this total, equaling the spending of the next seven nations with the largest military budgets—and many of those seven are our allies.

He contrasts this generous military funding with recent sharp cuts to U.S. humanitarian foreign aid:

> a 21 percent cut in Title II Food Aid at a time with a record number of fam-
> ines; a 20 percent cut in development assistance that funds such priorities
> as basic education, democracy-building initiatives, human rights, agri-
> culture, and employment; a 17 percent cut in U.S. refugee admissions at a
> time when the number of displaced people is at its highest since World War
> II; dramatic reductions in key global health programs, including a 13 per-
> cent cut in the fight against polio, a 13 percent cut in nutrition assistance,
> a 34 percent cut to an account for vulnerable children, a 19 percent cut for
> addressing tuberculosis, and many others.[27]

From the perspective of Catholic social thought, peace is not merely the absence of war, but a social condition in which structures and relationships of equality and justice are established. A shift in focus from just war to just peace necessitates, among other things, a shift in spending priorities and increased effort to prevent conflict through development aid and grassroots peacebuilding activities. Obviously, this approach would entail a dramatic reorientation of U.S. foreign policy. But this is precisely what Catholic social thought demands. Grounding politics in mercy rather than violence will disrupt the political status quo in the United States.[28]

A just peace approach prioritizes a **preventative** response to vio-
lence and seeks to build the conditions for peace by building a more just social order rather than focusing on a method for discerning when it is morally permissible to employ violence. Additionally, a just peace approach focuses on practices of **reconciliation** as a means of peace-making. Such practices resonate with the **restorative justice** model that we examined in Chapter 3. So, too, do they cohere with what we learned in Chapter 2 about the Jesuit Refugee Service, which has made reconciliation one of its strategic priorities. Practices of reconciliation combat xenophobia and racism in host countries. In countries of origin, practices of reconciliation are used to try to prevent conflict, and thus more migration. Catholic peacebuilding pursues reconciliation to prevent conflict by building relationships among diverse ethnic, racial, and religious groups, and, in the aftermath of armed conflict, seeking restorative justice among victims and perpetrators. The way to

just peace passes through reconciliation and restoration, the only true inhibitors to further violence.

Conclusion: Catholic Relief Services

Numerous Catholic organizations around the world integrate the just peace focus on development and reconciliation in their attempts to build a more enduring peace. These include Jesuit Refugee Service, Pax Christi, Sant' Egidio, and Catholic Relief Services (CRS). This last organization is of particular interest because it has explicitly adopted the just peace paradigm as its own framework for building more peaceable societies.[29]

CRS is the official humanitarian organization of the U.S. Catholic Church. It was founded in 1943 by the U.S. Catholic Bishops to provide relief for impoverished and vulnerable populations overseas; its original focus, given the time period, was war-ravaged Europe. Initially, CRS provided emergency relief to refugee populations, but the scope of its efforts broadened in the 1950s to include development and poverty prevention through training in agriculture, provision of microfinance, and other such endeavors.[30] The dual focus on emergency relief and development was broadened in 1994 in response to the genocide in Rwanda, which killed one million Rwandans, left 300,000 children orphaned and 500,000 women widowed, and turned three million people into refugees.[31]

CRS had been on the ground in Rwanda for over thirty years by 1994. Staff members had been aware of the nation's ethnic tensions, but sought to work around them.[32] At the time of the genocide, there were thirty CRS staff members in the country, fifteen of whom were Tutsis, the ethnic group on the receiving end of the genocide. Nine of the staff members and their families were murdered.[33] In response to the trauma of these events, CRS decided to reassess its worldwide development strategy. While painfully aware of these ethnic and racial tensions in countries like Rwanda, CRS had viewed its primary task as development, not reconciliation. The Rwandan genocide forced CRS to place more emphasis on examining the social and cultural realities that lead to conflict. CRS recognized that it could not fulfill its goal of serving the needs of the poorest and most vulnerable in the world if it failed to understand and respond to the structural dynamics that cause exclusion and violence.[34] To its charitable actions, CRS added a justice component.

CRS began to focus on peacebuilding as a central feature of its work. The CRS approach to peacebuilding integrates Paul VI's call for a renewed emphasis on just development as a means of promoting peace with practices of reconciliation to heal conflict. Consistent with Catholic social teaching on **subsidiarity**, which maintains that social needs and problems should be addressed by the most local body possible, CRS collaborates with local churches and community-based organizations on the ground to offer programming committed to peace and justice.

In 2018, CRS's "Justice and Peacebuilding" programs served over 2.8 million people in 34 countries. After the genocide, CRS partnered with the Catholic Church in Rwanda to train over 40,000 leaders in conflict resolution and peacebuilding.[35] Peacebuilders trained by CRS work within their local communities, where they seek out recently released prisoners accused of involvement in the genocide. They facilitate public examinations of conscience that encourage perpetrators to confess their crimes and to seek forgiveness from family members of the murdered.[36] Such work is being done in the Community Healing and Reconciliation Program at the Rugango parish in southern Rwanda. CRS partners with the Diocese of Butare to facilitate this program. Kerry Weber describes some concrete results: "Esperance M'Mugemana sits directly beside Fidele Mparikubwimana, who killed several members of her family during the genocide. She speaks calmly, and with quiet strength. 'When they said I could meet the person who killed my husband and family, I didn't want to meet him,' she says. 'But he came to ask me forgiveness. I told him, if you ask from deep within your heart, I forgive you.'"[37] Lest these brief statements make it sound as if the peace between M'Mugemana and Mparikubwimana was simple and easily effected, we should note the fourfold process that CRS used to facilitate it. The process involves justice, truth, mercy, and—then and only then—peace:

- **Justice**: Mparikubwimana spent eleven years in prison.
- **Truth:** Mparikubwimana confessed to M'Mugemana what he did.
- **Mercy:** Mparikubwimana asked for and received forgiveness from M'Mugemana.
- **Peace:** M'Mugemana and Mparikubwimana embark on a life in common that acknowledges past wrongs but nevertheless seeks reconciliation.

Justice, truth, mercy, and peace: the concrete interlocking of these four elements shows that if you want enduring peace, you need all of these to operate. The lesson of CRS is that development work is important, even vital. But more ingredients are needed for lasting peace.

In conclusion, we should note how starkly the approach of CRS contrasts with American militarism. CRS provides humanitarian aid, supports development efforts, and participates in the reconciling work of peacebuilding in response to conflict. From a Catholic perspective, U.S. militarism is deficient on multiple levels. John Paul II and Benedict XVI raised critical questions about whether the United States has fulfilled even the minimal demands of the just war criteria in their military engagements over the past forty years. Both have concluded that the United States' military involvement has not fulfilled them. But even more objections must be raised, beyond the just war paradigm. The framework of just peace calls into question the United States' decision to devote a disproportionate amount of its resources to military spending rather than development, peacebuilding, and reconciliation efforts. The country spends less than 3% of its discretionary budget on foreign aid (humanitarian, economic growth, democratic governance) and over 50% of its discretionary budget on defense. From a Catholic just peace perspective, this proportion of spending should be reversed or, at the very least, reweighted so that the majority of spending goes toward humanitarian aid and development.

While CRS hardly operates on the scale of the U.S. military, it does provide a viable, global alternative to it. Starting from the example of CRS, we can imagine a politics of mercy and just peace opposed to a politics of militarism and sacrifice. The case of CRS's activities in Rwanda demonstrates that a politics of mercy, little by little, can resolve conflict and bring reconciliation. U.S. militarism promises freedom while delivering ever more war; such is the lie of violence. With the politics of mercy, we catch glimpses of the truth, the truth called "just peace"—and the truth will set us free (Jn 8:32).

Notes

1   Amanda Macais, "America Has Spent 6.4 Trillion on Wars in the Middle East and
     Asia," CNBC, November 20, 2019, https://www.cnbc.com/2019/11/20/us-spent-
     6point4-trillion-on-middle-east-wars-since-2001-study.html.

2   Murtaza Hussain, "It's Time for America to Reckon with the Staggering Death Toll
     of the Post-9/11 Wars," *The Intercept*, November 19, 2018, https://theintercept
     .com/2018/11/19/civilian-casualties-us-war-on-terror/.

3   Richard Fontaine, "The Nonintervention Delusion," *Foreign Affairs*, November/
     December   2019,   https://www.foreignaffairs.com/articles/2019-10-15/
     nonintervention-delusion.

4   Alice Slater, "The US Has Military Bases in 80 Countries," *The Nation*, January 24,
     2018, https://www.thenation.com/article/the-us-has-military-bases-in-172
     -countries-all-of-them-must-close/.

5   Kimberly Amadeo, "U.S. Military Budget," *The New Balance*, April 22, 2019,
     https://www.thebalance.com/u-s-military-budget-components-challenges
     -growth-3306320.

6   David Tweed, "China Defense Spending Set to Rise," *Bloomberg*, March 4, 2019,
     https://www.bloomberg.com/news/articles/2019-03-05/china-s-military
     -spending-slows-as-economy-cools.

7   Nikhil Pal Singh, *Race and America's Long War* (Oakland: University of California
     Press, 2017), 3ff.

8   Quoted in Andrew Bacevich, *American Empire: The Realities and Consequences of
     U.S. Diplomacy* (Cambridge, MA: Harvard University Press, 2002), preface.

9   Pope Francis observes that "Jesus himself offers a 'manual' for this strategy of
     peacemaking in the Sermon on the Mount. The eight Beatitudes (see Mt 5:3–10)
     provide a portrait of the person we could describe as blessed, good and authen-
     tic. Blessed are the meek, Jesus tells us, the merciful and the peacemakers, those
     who are pure in heart, and those who hunger and thirst for justice." John Paul II,
     "Peace with God the Creator, Peace with All of Creation," http://w2.vatican.va/
     content/francesco/en/messages/peace/documents/papa-francesco_20161208_
     messaggio-l-giornata-mondiale-pace-2017.html#_ftnref4.

10   George Weigel adopts this position. See George Weigel, "The Catholic Difference: Getting 'Just-War' Straight," *Zenit*, October 13, 2001, https://zenit. org/articles/george-weigel-on-just-war-principles/.

11   See, for instance, Michael Baxter, "Just War and Pacifism: A 'Pacifist' Perspective in Seven Points," *Houston Catholic Worker Newsletter*, June 1, 2004, https://cjd .org/2004/06/01/just-war-and-pacifism-a-pacifist-perspective-in-seven-points/.

12   Paul VI, "Message of His Holiness Paul VI for the Observance of a Day of Peace," January 1, 1968, http://w2.vatican.va/content/paul-vi/en/messages/peace/ documents/hf_p-vi_mes_19671208_i-world-day-for-peace.html.

13   Paul VI, "Day of Peace," January 1, 1972, http://w2.vatican.va/content/paul-vi/en/ messages/peace/documents/hf_p-vi_mes_19711208_v-world-day-for-peace.html.

14   John Dear, "The Catholic Campaign to End Iraq War," *National Catholic Reporter*, August 21, 2017, https://www.ncronline.org/blogs/road-peace/ catholic-campaign-end-iraq-war.

15   It is important to note that Francis continues to affirm the need in rare circumstances to use violence to defend the common good: "governments cannot be denied the right to legitimate defense once every means of peaceful settlement has been exhausted." But this is the only comment in Francis's speeches and messages on war and conflict in which he invokes the ongoing relevance of the just war tradition.

16   Pope Francis, "Message of His Holiness Pope Francis for the Fiftieth World Day of Peace," January 1, 2019, https://w2.vatican.va/content/francesco/en/messages/ peace/documents/papa-francesco_20161208_messaggio-l-giornata-mondiale- pace-2017.html#_ftnref15.

17   Lisa Sowle Cahill, *Blessed Are the Peacemakers: Pacifism, Just War, and Peacebuilding* (Minneapolis. MN: Fortress Press, 2019), 316.

18   The following analysis is based on Keenan, *The Works of Mercy*, 77–80. All references to social crises are ours, not Keenan's.

19   Keenan, *The Works of Mercy*, 80.

20   Hartford Catholic Worker, "We Are the Hartford Catholic Worker," video, https:// hartfordcatholicworker.org/our-history/, 20:04–20:16. The Hartford Catholic Worker was co-founded by Jackie Allen-Douçot, Christopher Allen-Douçot, and Brian Kavanagh in 1992.

21   For more information, see an article from the Dorothy Day archives at
     Marquette University: "Civil Defense Drill Protests: Dorothy Day and Friends Sit
     in for Peace," April 2009, https://www.marquette.edu/library/archives/News/
     spotlight/04-2009.php.

22   Dorothy Day, *Selected Writings: By Little and By Little*, edited with an introduction
     by Robert Ellsberg (Maryknoll, NY: Orbis Books, 2005), 280.

23   Paul Magno, "The Plowshares Anti-Nuclear Movement at 35: A Next
     Generation?" *Bulletin of Atomic Scientists* 72, no. 2 (2016): 85–88, at 86.

24   See the website of the Kings Bay Plowshares 7: https://kingsbayplowshares7.org/.

25   Pope Francis, "Vigil of Prayer for Peace," September 7, 2013, http://www.vatican
     .va/content/francesco/en/homilies/2013/documents/papa-francesco_
     20130907_veglia-pace.html.

26   Pope Francis, "Message of His Holiness Pope Francis for the Fiftieth World Day
     of Peace."

27   Cardinal Blase J. Cupich, "Witnessing to a Consistent Ethic of Solidarity,"
     Commonweal, May 19, 2017, https://www.commonwealmagazine.org/cardinal-blase-
     cupich-signs-times.

28   Gerald Schlabach, "Just War? Enough Already," *Commonweal*, May 31, 2017, https://
     www.commonwealmagazine.org/just-war-0: "Though we seem stuck with a seman-
     tically negative term, active nonviolence is in fact a positive. Within a just-peace
     framework, it is certainly more than protest or civil resistance. It is creative diplo-
     macy. It is behind-the-scenes conflict transformation of the sort that the Vatican
     and the Colombian church have brought to fruition in a breakthrough peace accord
     between guerrillas and the government. It is the training of local communities and
     regional leaders in processes of restorative justice, followed by the institutionaliz-
     ing of those processes in legal systems. It is demilitarized police forces. It is trauma
     healing that diverts cycles of violence in devastated communities around the world,
     and supports veterans in deed, not merely with slogans."

29   See the essays in *Pursuing Just Peace*, edited by Mark M. Rogers, Tom Bamat, and
     Julie Ideh (Baltimore, MD: Catholic Relief Services, 2008).

30   William R. Headley and Reina C. Neufeldt, "Catholic Relief Services: Catholic
     Peacebuilding in Practice," in *Peacebuilding: Catholic Theology, Ethics, and Praxis*,

edited by Robert Schreiter, Scott Appleby, and Gerard Powers (Maryknoll, NY: Orbis Books, 2010), 125–54.

31 Ron Lajoie, "To Forgive: Rwanda Two Decades after the Genocide," *Catholic New York*, November 13, 2013, http://cny.org/stories/to-forgive-rwanda-two-decades-after-the-genocide,10219.

32 Scott Appleby, *The Ambivalence of the Sacred: Religion, Violence, and Reconciliation* (Lanham, MD: Rowman & Littlefield, 2000), 52.

33 Kerry Weber, "Shadowed by Tragedy: Rwanda Strives to Rise above a History of Horror," *America*, April 7, 2014, https://www.americamagazine.org/issue/shadowed-tragedy#.

34 Carolyn Woo, "Blessed Are the Peacemakers," *Catholic Relief Services*, https://www.crs.org/media-center/carolyn-woo%E2%80%99s-cns-column-blessed-are-peacemakers.

35 Michelle Bauman, "Twenty Years after Genocide, Church Helps Rwanda Heal," *Catholic News Agency*, April 7, 2014, https://www.catholicnewsagency.com/news/twenty-years-after-rwandan-genocide-church-helps-bring-healing.

36 Jeffrey Odell Korgen, "Forgiveness Unbound: Reconciliation Education Is Helping Rwanda to Heal," *America*, September 10, 2007, https://www.americamagazine.org/issue/624/article/forgiveness-unbound.

37 Weber, "Shadowed by Tragedy: Rwanda Strives to Rise above a History of Horror."

CHAPTER 5

Ecology

Introduction

Hurricane Maria made landfall in Puerto Rico on September 20, 2017. It devastated the island, leaving hundreds of thousands of people hungry and thirsty, suffering through hot nights and hotter days, and sitting on the brink of contracting a variety of illnesses. During the same hurricane, the Caribbean island of Dominica suffered catastrophic damage, with nearly every structure destroyed. Less than two weeks earlier, Hurricane Irma had leveled another Caribbean island, Barbuda, rendering it effectively uninhabitable. Mere days before, the fifth-largest metropolitan area in the United States, Houston, was inundated by unprecedented flooding, overwhelming what turned out to be a woefully insufficient emergency preparedness infrastructure.

In addition to the loss of homes and immediate loss of life in all of these places, several factors made the historic 2017 hurricane and fire season even more troubling. First, 2017 seems to have been a harbinger of things to come, as climate scientists contend that **anthropogenic climate change** (human-caused shifts in global, long-term weather patterns caused mainly through emission of greenhouse gases from the burning of fossil fuels) will, by the twenty-first century's end, bring hurricanes with more intensity and higher rainfall rates than present-day hurricanes.[1] What was virtually unprecedented in 2017 may become commonplace later in the century. Second, worse storms will bring long-term health risks, as did Hurricane Irma in Florida, where infrastructure was overwhelmed, releasing flesh-eating bacteria from the Gulf of Mexico into city streets, raw sewage (by the millions of gallons) into neighborhoods, mold into households, and carcinogenic pollution out of petrochemical plants into all the places people live.[2] There is little reason to believe that this will not happen again with the next intense storm. Third, we can justifiably lack confidence that such crises will be averted because of the current condition of governments, whether federal, state, or municipal. The failure of levees, inadequacy (or absence) of evacuation routes, and, quite simply, a landscape dominated by too much pavement, exposed a key failure of government: it now exists not to safeguard public goods and livelihoods, but to ensure profits for businesses (in the case of Houston, housing developers).[3] Fourth, the hurricanes of 2017 laid bare what drives the contemporary world—often to its own destruction. In the immediate aftermath of Hurricane Maria, U.S. President Donald Trump blamed Puerto Ricans for their own victimization, citing the island's public debt as a major driver of their suffering.[4] Relatedly, in the financial press, rather than discussing the gravity of the humanitarian crisis in Puerto Rico, hedge fund managers wrung their hands over the possibility that their investment in Puerto Rican municipal bonds may go bust.[5] These are the types of attitudes and behaviors that Francis has in mind when he talks about wealth inequality as the root of all social ills.

With the hurricane season of 2017, we discovered a nexus of anthropogenic climate change: massive risks to home, health, and life itself; a diminished public will to care for one another (represented by governments facilitating private profit); and a financialized mentality that views crises as opportunities for earning a buck, or, in Puerto Rico's case, for worrying about how bucks may be lost. We see the results of human violence toward the earth. We detect the unwillingness of some people to reject this violence, except to lament its negative effects on their investment portfolios.

The 2017 hurricane season can and should be seen as nature hitting back at people. This is not to personalize "nature," but to be honest about what natural science has taught us about the delicate balance of life and the unlikelihood that there would be life at all (Earth is still the only known planet out of billions to support life), but also the tendency of life to come roaring back when placed under threat. Jesus teaches that "all who take the sword will perish by the sword" (Mt 26:52). Since the dawning of industrial economies in the eighteenth century, up through the superhumanly scaled global consumption of energy in the twenty-first, humans have taken the sword of fossil fuels. With hope, we will not perish. But a massive conversion of our hearts, habits, governments, markets, and societies must occur, should we evade the sword that nature may wield in our direction.

Crisis

The fossil fuel economy is a tremendous discovery in human history, even geological history. It has generated incredible amounts of wealth and human comfort beyond what anyone could have envisioned even a few hundred years ago. But the collateral damage is also immense. When human beings discovered fossil fuels beneath the earth's surface and began to harness them as a potent form of energy, there was little understanding of the impact it would have on modern society—both for good and for ill. For the first few hundred years it was viewed as an unambiguous good that contributed positively to human progress. It was not until 1956, in a *New York Times* article, that the phenomenon of climate change received public attention, and not until the late 1980s that a forceful case was made that burning fossil fuels and releasing carbon dioxide (CO_2) into the atmosphere had an adverse impact on the environment.[6] While a certain level of CO_2 is necessary in order to preserve a level of warmth on the planet that makes it hospitable to life, there is also a tipping point at which an excessive concentration of CO_2 in the atmosphere warms the planet beyond its capacity to continue to sustain that life. CO_2 and other greenhouse gases trap the heat of the sun, much as the glass exterior of a greenhouse serves to trap heat inside. At a certain point, however, these greenhouse gases begin to contribute to the phenomenon known as global warming or climate change. The concentration of CO_2 in the atmosphere has increased rapidly since the Industrial Revolution, from 275 parts per million (ppm) in the 1700s to 414 ppm in 2019. The 414 ppm rate is a dramatic departure from the stable level that has made the earth hospitable to life for millions of years. In fact, scientists maintain that the current level of CO_2 in the atmosphere is the highest in approximately three million years.

What is even more dramatic than this extraordinary rise in the level of CO_2 in the atmosphere is the fact that the majority of it has taken place in the past thirty years. As David Wallace-Wells describes in *The Uninhabitable Earth*, over half of the CO_2 that humans have released into the atmosphere since the harnessing of fossil fuels in the early 1700s has taken place since the first episode of *Seinfeld* aired. That means that over half of the total CO_2 emissions humans have released into the environment have occurred since 1989. Since the end of World War II, the number is 85%.[7] This unprecedented release of CO_2 into the atmosphere has resulted in a rapid increase in global average temperatures. Since the dawn of the Industrial Revolution, global average temperatures have risen approximately one degree Celsius (1.8 degrees Fahrenheit). Climatologists have long argued that the consequences will be dire if the increase in global average temperatures reaches two degrees. The problem is that if current trends continue, we are projected to reach two degrees before the year 2050. Even more seriously, two degrees appears to be the floor rather than the ceiling when it comes to warming. (The United Nations projects that we will arrive at 4.3 degrees of warming by the end of the century.) Beyond two degrees, the scenarios are apocalyptic. Wallace-Wells puts it starkly: "Absent a significant adjustment to how billions of humans conduct their lives, parts of the Earth will likely become close to uninhabitable, and other parts horrifically inhospitable, as soon as the end of this century."[8] He outlines several direct threats to human and non-human life from two degrees or more of warming, among them death from direct heat, widespread crop failure, the release of diseases frozen in Arctic ice and the northward movement of tropical diseases, declining air quality, broadening and intensifying social conflicts, reduced economic output, and chemical changes to ocean composition (acidification, underoxygenation, and increased prevalence of hydrogen sulfide—significant because oceans support the most life on earth). The picture is certainly bleak. A planet two degrees warmer would pose grave difficulties for human and non-human life.

Further complicating the situation is the fact that the three most widespread responses of the general public promise little by way of substantive action to rectify this crisis. These three common responses are denialism, technocracy, and apathy.

Climate **denialism** is a distinctive worldview in the United States that rejects the claims made by the scientific community that a relationship exists between human activity and the changing climate. Climate denialists suggest that the recent shifts in the earth's climate are part of its natural cycle of warming and cooling over its four-billion-year history. Notably, 99% of scientists and virtually every climatologist not funded by oil companies rejects these claims.[9] There is widespread consensus among scientists that the global rise in average temperatures is anthropogenic, and this consensus has been accepted in official Catholic social teaching.

A broad base of support for denialism has been created by a combustible mix of proponents of the free market who oppose state intervention in the economy, religious suspicion about scientific truth claims, and fossil fuel companies seeking to protect their business models. Proponents of the free market fear that acknowledgment of climate science would result in a severe governmental intrusion into the market in order to regulate and make economic activity more ecologically sustainable. In the United States, evangelical Christians—and even some Catholics—have provided a populist base of support for denialism. Many evangelicals and Catholics distrust scientists because of the rejection of creationism among the scientific community, so skepticism regarding climate science is hardly surprising. Fossil fuel companies have hired various "experts" (often from think tanks) to sow doubt in the public concerning the relationship between burning fossil fuels and climate change. There is precedent for this. Tobacco companies funded research to cast doubt on the relation between smoking and lung cancer by undermining the legitimacy of scientific and public health organizations. The aim was to create confusion in the public so as to protect the profits of the tobacco industry. In *Merchants of Doubt*, Naomi Oreskes and Erik Conway document how the fossil fuel industry adopted a similar strategy by funding research that casts doubt on the relationship between human activity and climate change.[10] Because of the shared effort on the part of free marketers, some religious people, and fossil fuel companies, about one-third of the U.S. population expresses support for a denialist position regarding climate change.

There are other options for reacting to climate change that accept the scientific consensus but share with denialists a hesitancy with regard to broad societal and economic change in response to it. A wide swath of the U.S. population, represented quite often by Democratic politicians, follows the **technocratic paradigm** that Francis criticizes in *Laudato Si'* (*LS*, 101, 106, 109, 111, 112, 122). This model for human thinking and action holds that all problems can be solved through technology (whether by machines, information technology, biotechnology, or other instruments of human ingenuity). The technocratic paradigm advocates a variety of market-based and/or technological means to address climate change. Famous among them has been the development of pollution permits, which would allow companies to pollute a certain amount, above which they could not go unless they purchased more permits. This idea is commonly referred to as "cap and trade," since carbon and other emissions are capped at a certain limit, and permits are traded to exceed this amount. Little evidence has been found that this strategy would reduce harmful emissions. A similar strategy has been adopted by technology firms and capitalists like Elon Musk, founder of the electric car company Tesla. Rather than attempting to discover different ways that society and infrastructure could be reorganized to make transportation more sustainable, new technologies that offer direct replacement (without any displacement) of existing technologies are seen as the way forward. Cars remain on roadways. Now they will be electric. Whether with cap and trade or electric cars, the technocratic way of responding to climate change presupposes one crucial thing: human life as we know it in highly developed economies must remain exactly as it is, with its same high levels of consumption, and the only changes we can make are small tweaks, tinkering with markets and technology. As with climate denialism, the result of such a presupposition is no serious action to address climate change.

Perhaps the most widespread response to the crisis has been apathy or a lack of concern. Climate change is the type of challenge that makes apathy seem like an obvious or even inevitable response. It often feels as though the effects of climate change will be experienced in the distant future and only by people from other countries or regions of one's own country. Furthermore, while virtually every person contributes to climate change in daily life, there is no specific agent that can be easily identified as its cause. The particular challenge that the slow violence of climate change poses is that there aren't obvious perpetrators, as with the rapid violence of war. This, along with the fact that humans are not engineered to respond to complex, slow-moving threats, makes it quite difficult to generate the type of urgency that is needed to respond to what is an unparalleled threat in human history.

While denialism, the technocratic paradigm, and apathy represent the three most common responses—or non-responses—to climate change in the United States, it is worth emphasizing here that an overwhelming response is required, precisely because of the unique way in which climate change intersects with the other pressing issues we have explored: inequality, racism, and political violence. How, specifically, do these crises intersect with climate change in view of Francis's claim that "everything is connected"?

- **Inequality**: Francis has argued that the responsibility of Catholics is to hear both the cry of the earth and the cry of the poor (*LS*, 49). The most catastrophic effects of climate change will be experienced by the global poor. The painful paradox of this situation is that the carbon footprint of this population is comparatively small in relation to affluent populations in Europe and the United States. In *Laudato Si'*, Francis quotes the New Zealand bishops who ask what the commandment "Thou shall not kill" means when "twenty percent of the world's population consumes resources at a rate that robs the poor nations and future generations of what they need to survive" (*LS*, 95).

- **Environmental racism**: The reality by which poor communities of color experience the most extreme effects of environmental degradation. Communities of color are often located in **sacrifice zones**, or places deemed disposable on the path toward economic progress. Federal and state governments often place housing projects for poor communities of color next to petrochemical plants, oil refineries, and locations vulnerable to natural disasters. For example, the African American community in New Orleans suffered most intensely as a result of Hurricane Katrina (2004) because historic patterns of structural racism (economic disempowerment, housing discrimination, lack of access to transportation and public goods) made their communities more vulnerable to natural disasters. Furthermore, the lack of a quick and effective governmental response to Hurricane Katrina and Hurricane Maria in Puerto Rico demonstrates the way in which the U.S. government exhibits a **racially selective indifference**, or an inability to feel the suffering of others based on their skin pigmentation and/or social location.

Certainly such indifference has applied to the experience of displacement, deprivation, and social suffering among communities of color in the United States.[11]

- **Migration:** The intensification of extreme weather events (droughts, flooding, unbearable heat, hurricanes) has created a new category of people: climate migrants (or climate refugees). These persons have been displaced from their land as a result of the intensification of extreme weather events. Right now there are 272 million global migrants who have left their home because of violent conflict, poverty, persecution, and extreme weather. The World Bank recently estimated that there will be 143 million climate migrants in Latin America, sub-Saharan Africa, and Southeast Asia alone by 2050.[12]

- **War:** We criticized American militarism in the previous chapter as an institutional structure that sacrifices lives in the name of national security. The American military-industrial complex is also the single greatest institutional emitter of fossil fuels in the world. The data suggest that the U.S. military's total CO_2 output exceeds that of entire countries with populations over 10 million—for example, Sweden and Portugal.[13]

We can see that because these crises intersect with and amplify each other, it is a grave error to treat them as separate or isolated. This is a major reason why we advocate a politics of mercy: the works of mercy reimagined as a politics serves as a Catholic response to the multifaceted challenges of inequality, racism, and violence.

Thus far our discussion of the climate crisis has been mostly secular. It is worth explaining how a Catholic theological way of seeing can contribute something distinctive to the statement of the problem and how to respond to it. Francis's *Laudato Si'* exemplifies the difference that theology can make. He agrees with secular diagnoses of what ails us, but he offers specifically Catholic notes of hope. He expresses it this way: "The Creator does not abandon us; he never forsakes his loving plan or repents of having created us. Humanity still has the ability to work together in building our common home" (*LS*, 13). While there are plenty of secular groups and individuals who would agree with the latter statement, the former is distinctly Catholic. Francis is saying not only that time and human capability are on the side of those who want to mitigate climate change's effects, but also that the author of reality itself is on our side. He updates Paul's encouragement of the early Roman church: "If God is for us, who can be against us?" (Rom 8:31). This may not seem like much, but given the often fiercely negative forecasts of secular—and even religious—writers about climate change, which result in hopelessness and apathy, genuine hope of any sort should not be dismissed. We describe the reasons for hope in the face of a very dire situation in the remainder of this chapter.

Catholic Social Thought

We promised in Chapter 1 that we would return to the Christian doctrine of **creation**. The common move in addressing our ecological crisis is to remind people that our world (indeed our universe) is God's creation, and to make a plea that people treat it as such, rather than treating it violently. We echo that reminder and plea here. But we must also reflect on the idea of the **Incarnation**, Jesus Christ's taking on of human flesh (Latin: *caro*, *carnis*), which means that God has entered creation, or made God's dwelling among us (Jn 1:14) in the person of Jesus. The fact that God did this should indelibly mark Catholic thought and life.

In Chapter 1, we referenced several biblical texts out of which the Catholic theology of creation has developed. From this biblical material we learn that non-human creation as a whole and in each of its parts has dignity that can be favorably compared to human dignity. This dignity is defined by what creation is—namely, good in itself (Gen 1:4, 10, 12, 18, 21, 25, 31). This dignity also constitutes a task: to praise God. The prayer of Azariah in the Book of Daniel is a prime example of this. The prayer exhorts all creatures to bless the Lord. It begins, "Bless the Lord, all you works of the Lord, / Praise and exalt him above all forever" (Dn 3:57). It then goes through all manner of creatures, from the inanimate (sun, moon, stars, rain, dew, winds, fire, snow, lightning and clouds, seasons, night and day, mountains and hills, plants that grow from the ground) to the animate (whales and dwellers of the seas, birds of the air, wild animals and cattle, all people on earth), encouraging them to praise the God who made them (Dn 3:58–82). In order for creation to continue to be what it is (good) and to do what it is made to do (glorify and praise God), it must be treated peacefully, without the violence that we tend to inflict upon it today.

Recent papal teaching has taken these biblical insights seriously. Paul VI, with his statements on the environment in the apostolic letter *Octogesima Adveniens* (1971) and a message to the 1972 United Nations Conference on the Environment, was the first pope to express explicit concern with the environment.[14] His brief references to advancing planetary crisis have been augmented by his successors, with, for example, "Peace with God the Creator, Peace with All of Creation" (John Paul II, 1990), *In the Beginning: A Catholic Understanding of the Story of Creation and Fall* (Benedict XVI, 1985), and *Laudato Si'* (Francis, 2015). John Paul's reflection on the World Day of Peace draws the link between the Catholic doctrine of creation and the ecological crisis. It marks this crisis as a moral one that is characterized by "the indiscriminate application of advances in science and technology," with improper attention to responsibility and future consequences.[15] John Paul proposes recovering the ideas of a "harmonious universe" and "common heritage" as impetus to a salutary vision and shared work geared toward healing the earth.[16] Benedict XVI's message for the World Day of Peace in 2010, "If You Want to Cultivate Peace, Protect Creation," summed up his long-standing emphasis on this title theme in his *In the Beginning* and *Caritas in Veritate*. He advocates recognizing the world as *creation*, which has become difficult in an age dominated by scientific thinking and capitalist production.[17] Such recognition would involve seeing the world as "a wondrous work of the Creator containing a 'grammar' which sets forth ends and criteria for its wise use, not its reckless exploitation" (*CV*, 48). In *Laudato Si'*, Francis deepens this papal critique of a technological and market-driven comportment toward the natural world, and offers a constructive template for following the Gospel of Creation (*LS*, 62–100). Francis reminds his readers that Catholicism involves **sacramental** engagement with the natural world, seeing it as a substantial sign of God's presence. Francis explains: "The universe unfolds in God, who fills it completely. Hence, there is a mystical meaning to be found in a leaf, in a mountain trail, in a dewdrop, in a poor person's face. The ideal is not only to pass from the exterior to the interior to discover the action of God in the soul, but also to discover God in all things" (*LS*, 233).

The popes' teachings on creation, including their rejection of violence toward and domination of nature, point to a Catholic ethos rooted in healing. God's merciful love brings God to create, so God may share God's love with another; so, too, does God's mercy recognize the pain in this broken "other" and meet it with saving care. Francis points out that Jesus lived in full harmony with creation, even so much that the winds and sea obeyed him (*LS*, 98). Christ's life on earth testified to what was true from creation's beginning, that "all things have been created through him and for him" (Col 1:16). It testified to what will be true at its end, when the Son will hand all things over to the Father, "so that 'God may be everything to every one'" (1 Cor 15:28). And it testified to what is true of all things in creation now: that "the risen One is mysteriously holding them to himself and directing them towards fullness as their end" (*LS*, 100). As human beings persist in breaking their relationship with creation by willfully destroying it, God is at work in Jesus Christ addressing its wounds with mercy. Those who follow Christ are called, in turn, to work here and now for a healthier environment. This work must be facilitated and energized by "ecological conversion" (*LS*, 216–21), which would turn away from violence against creation and toward the Christic, "sublime fraternity with all creation which Saint Francis of Assisi so radiantly embodied" (*LS*, 221).

What we have already seen in the papal writings should suggest the intimate connection between the doctrine of creation and **Christology**, the area of theology that examines the person and mission of Jesus Christ. The Incarnation, the central Christological idea, has profound implications for how Christians see and relate to God's creation. The Son of God entered into creation and "was manifested in the flesh" (1 Tim 3:16). This is a tremendous display of divine solidarity with all that God has made, but also a transformative event, in which God pours out new life into a wounded and fractured world. The incarnation as solidarity and transformation must be understood in tandem with the Paschal Mystery of Christ's death, resurrection, and ascension, since the Paschal Mystery shows the extent of God's entrance into creation: from lowly birth (Mt 1:18–25; Lk 2:1–7) all the way through shameful death (Mk 15:25–32) and descent into the "lower regions of the earth" (Eph 4:9). The God of all and of heavenly glory reaches into the plainest and most desolate reaches of creation to save it all. God's solidarity and transformative activity is witnessed to in Paul's theology of baptism. Paul tells the new Christians at Corinth that, by being initiated into the life of Christ, they have become a new creation (2 Cor 5:17).

What happens to them is unified with what happens to the wider creation. Whatever Christ touches—and Christ touches all by making his dwelling among us (Jn 1:14) and dying for all (2 Cor 5:15)—is renewed, turned back toward the God who made it. All that we have just described is what Paul calls the "pillar and foundation of truth" (1 Tim 3:15), or what we could name the bedrock commitments of Catholic life.

Theologians Niels Gregersen, Elizabeth Johnson, and Denis Edwards have reflected on the meaning of this pillar and foundation of truth in light of recent ecological science. Gregersen coins the term **deep incarnation**, by which he means Christ's entrance into creation to the point of biological existence's very tissue, or the system of nature. He means with this idea to aid our understanding of how Christian belief in God's mercy squares (or doesn't) with the often ruthless character of evolution.[18] According to Johnson, the idea points to "the radical divine reach in Christ through human flesh all the way down into the living web of organic life with its growth and decay, amid the wider processes of evolving nature that beget and sustain life."[19] Johnson and Edwards use Gregersen's term to discover how a reframed understanding of Christ's incarnation can impel Christians' ecological thinking and action.[20]

Johnson's elaboration of deep incarnation gives concrete expression to who Jesus is and what he, as God incarnate, can mean for us in an era of new ecological awareness. She writes: "As a creature of the earth, Jesus was a complex living unit of minerals and fluids, an item in the carbon, oxygen, and nitrogen cycles. The atoms comprising his body were once part of other creatures. The genetic structure of the cells in his body were kin to the flowers, fish, frogs, finches, foxes, the whole community of life that descended from common ancestors in the ancient seas."[21] Jesus was plugged into the structures and cycles of nature; he shared genetic material and the cellular makeup of other organisms; minerals and nutrients sustained him and passed through him as he ate, drank, and excreted; he existed in space-time; he abided in a Mediterranean climate; he participated in all aspects of earthly life. Johnson finds resonance between these insights and Paul's exhortation to the Colossians: "And you who once were alienated and hostile in mind because of evil deeds, he has now reconciled in his fleshly body through his death, to present you holy, without blemish, irreproachable before [God], provided that you persevere in the faith, firmly grounded, stable, and not shifting from the hope of the gospel that you heard, which has been preached to every creature under heaven" (Col 1:21–23). The gospel is not only preached to every creature, but touches every creature in person through Jesus Christ. Johnson finishes the thought, now with reference to Jesus's resurrection, which is the culminating point of the mystery of his incarnation and death: "One with the flesh of the earth, Jesus Christ risen embodies the ultimate hope of all creatures in creation. The coming final transformation of history will be the salvation of everything, including the groaning community of life [Rom 8:19–23], brought into communion with the God of love."[22]

This means that Christ's incarnation should not only be the starting point for Christian thinking about creation and how human persons should behave within and toward it. It also means that Christ's incarnation is the *goal* of creation and our attitudes and actions within and toward creation. If creation's goal is resurrection, and if Christ has already ushered the resurrection into creation (by rising from the dead within it), then people should act like it. They should act like creation is a realm of resurrection, not of death; of abundant life, not of scarcity and desperation.

We suggested earlier in this book that the global economy, which tends toward extreme inequality, must be redirected toward the goal of human beings living out their call to grandeur and glorifying God. We have likewise contended that racist structures, practices, and attitudes must be rejected as instruments of death that are unacceptable to people who have taken on the mind of Christ and who aim to live in anticipation of resurrected life here and now. We have contrasted warmaking with the Catholic vocation to peacebuilding, to continuing the resurrected life of Christ, and to breathing with the same Spirit that he bestowed upon his earliest disciples. A theological response to our era of ecological crisis should weave together all these themes, while bringing them to their widest and deepest application. All creation must be regarded as called to a life of grandeur and glorification; all creation must be treated as if death were not its master; all creation must be dealt with peacefully.

These are, for sure, tall orders. These imperatives may seem impossible and inattentive to the complexities of living in a sinful and broken world. These are difficult teachings. We could easily ask, as did those who heard Jesus's self-description as the Bread of Life, "Who can accept them?" (Jn 6:60). But taking the doctrines of creation and deep incarnation seriously leads to these prescriptions. As we shall see in the next section on the politics of mercy, we can find Catholics attempting, with much success, to observe them.

Before we embark on that section, though, let us return to the idea of the **universal destination of goods**, which we introduced in Chapter 1 in response to the crisis of inequality. With respect to climate change, another aspect of the teaching on universal destination of goods appears. That is, when a universal problem—a crisis of global magnitude—occurs, that problem must be recognized as affecting everyone and unavoidable by everyone. By that we mean that private individuals and comparatively smaller groups must not try to insulate themselves from a problem at the expense of others. Such behaviors and societal structures are becoming more prevalent. People and groups attempt to evade climate change's effects privately, whether through economic means such as purchasing exotic forms of disaster insurance or hiring private fire departments to extinguish more frequent forest fires, or through political means, such as resisting immigration, thus barring entry to climate refugees. If a politics of mercy is to be implemented, it has to take the form of radical efforts to turn the tide from private hoarding of creation and avoiding of problems toward common sharing of creation and acting to mitigate problems. This will include, we have been hinting, shared adjustment of lives and livelihoods to the climate crisis. Private comforts, luxuries, and habits of transportation, production, and consumption must give way, so that common discomforts—including death—are not shared.

The Politics of Mercy

The politics of mercy as it applies to climate change focuses on two spiritual works of mercy, **praying for the living** and **caring for creation**, as well as one corporal work of mercy, **visiting the sick**. Praying for the living in our era of climate, extinction, and other environmental crises means supplicating God for protection of life amid advancing slow violence and for ecological conversion to love for creation as a good in itself and as elevated by Christ. Visiting the sick in our era applies to healing the earth as well as attending to those communities sickened by the destruction of our common home. This entails the need for radical forms of direct action, as well as an attempt to respond structurally to the ecological debt incurred by affluent nations, especially the wealthiest individuals within them, that have contributed disproportionately to the current crisis.

Spiritual Works: Pray for the Living and Care for Creation

Chapter 4 presented the seventh spiritual work of mercy, **praying for the living and the dead**, as the first key ingredient to a nonviolent politics of mercy. We explained that we would divide this work of mercy into prayer for the dead, which could address the crisis of war, and prayer for the living, which may address the crisis of climate change. From James Keenan we gained the threefold distinction of prayer as **effective**, **unitive**, and **transformative**. Here we contend that the spiritual work of praying for the living can open a politics of mercy that responds to climate change, because such prayer (a) begs God to preserve life from the mass extinction that climate change threatens (and has already begun to inflict); (b) draws its practitioner near to all life on earth; and (c) enters into climate chaos to find where God may be encountered there, transforming this chaos from within.

We must recall that the spiritual work of praying for the living is a prayer of **supplication**, of pleading with God. Such pleading is especially necessary in the face of a coming climate cataclysm. The type of prayer that we discover in the Psalms, where the psalmist cries out to God while surrounded by enemies (Ps 22:11–18) or facing impending death (Ps 88:2–7), seems ever more appropriate. Keenan points out that prayer, in order to be effective, must be concrete. Effective prayer for the living in an age of climate violence should include specific petitions: that people affirm and not deny the reality of anthropogenic climate change, that people be given the hope they need to overcome apathy before such a monumental crisis, and that we all be given new hearts to replace the hardened hearts that allow us to participate in ecocide. Placing these prayers persistently before our God can help Catholics commence the arduous work of acting charitably in cleaning up local areas; putting sustainability into practice; dismantling ecocidal social, economic, and political structures; and fashioning new infrastructures of health and life. Also aiding such effort should be unitive prayer, the kind of prayer that supplicates God for greater awareness that everything in creation is connected, because God made all things (Rev 4:11). Catholics must honor God through all the things God has made—ourselves included. Effective and unitive prayer for the living should bring those who pray to a transformative encounter in prayer with a God of love, the Creator as a loving spouse (Is 54:5), who invites all the living into a partnership of rebuilding our common home.

To the seventh spiritual work of mercy we may add an eighth. Francis has suggested that the climate crisis necessitates the articulation of a new work of mercy: care for our common home. In 2015, as part of a joint initiative with Ecumenical Patriarch Bartholomew of the Orthodox Church, Francis declared that September 1 of each year would be the World Day of Prayer for the Care of Creation.[23] The following September 1, he made the case for the new work of mercy to complement the other fourteen.[24] He locates this work among the seven spiritual works of mercy—this work calls Catholics into a relationship of "grateful contemplation of God's world which allows" them "to discover in each thing a teaching which God wishes to hand on to us"—and the corporal works—it "requires simple daily gestures which break with the logic of violence, exploitation and selfishness and makes itself felt in every action that seeks to build a better world." This work of mercy is comprehensive, covering all human and even non-human life; thus it points toward justice, but in keeping with the best of Catholic spirituality, it stems from charitable actions in the everyday. We move, then, from the spiritual works of prayer for the living and care for our common home, to the charity dimension of a politics of mercy.

Charity: Visit the Sick

Jesus's first miracle in the Synoptic Gospels is healing the sick (Mk 1:21–31; Lk 4:31–39; Mt 4:23). On the basis of the scriptural evidence, it appears that attending to the sick and curing those afflicted with disease was central to Jesus's ministry. It is little wonder, then, that visiting the sick would become a central practice of mercy throughout the church's 2,000-year history, from the earliest apostles (Mt 10:1; Mk 16:18; Lk 9:1; Acts 5:12–16, 28:8–9; 1 Cor 12:9) through the present-day Catholic operation of hospitals and health-care organizations. We must also remember that, beginning with the scriptures, Catholics have turned to metaphors of healing to explicate salvation in Christ, most notably with the Christological reading of Isaiah 53:5, "by his wounds we were healed" (1 Pet 2:24). Benedict XVI evoked this passage in his message for the 2011 World Day of the Sick. And in view of extreme sickness of the planet—in *Laudato Si'*, Francis observed that we have turned creation into "an immense pile of filth" (*LS*, 21)—we think it fitting to apply the work of mercy of visiting the sick even more widely to the environmental crisis. We choose here to continue to reflect on **visiting the sick** from an environmental perspective and to reimagine what it means to visit and heal the sick in an age of environmental destruction. It entails not only direct restoration to health (which is needed), but also protection of those harmed and sickened by the ill effects of climate change.

Visiting the sick as a form of direct action must first entail a robust recommitment to truth, which at its most basic level involves contesting the widely disseminated idea that there is no relationship between human activity and environmental destruction. Even in the wake of *Laudato Si'*, one-third of Catholics in the United States deny that climate change is caused by human beings. In *Laudato Si'*, Francis emphasized the centrality of "ecological education" as a formative environmental practice urgently needed to confront this collective crisis. His conception of this "education" is expansive, extending beyond simply introducing Catholics to the basic scientific facts of environmental degradation. It includes aesthetic and sacramental formation that enables individuals "to see and appreciate beauty" and to "reject self-interested pragmatism" (*LS*, 215).

Additionally, Francis proposes a series of practices that range from lifestyle changes (*LS*, 203–8) and voluntary simplicity and limiting consumption (*LS*, 209–10), to individual and community action (*LS*, 216–20). For example, taking responsibility for a specific piece of land is a significant response to the climate crisis from a Catholic perspective. Francis contends that while these localized acts appear small, they do constitute an integral feature of the "bold cultural revolution" (*LS*, 114) needed to respond to the climate crisis at the levels of civil society and political and economic life. Some popular contemporary approaches to the climate crisis posit that a structural remedy alone is sufficient. This is a pervasive position on the political left in which certain forms of direct action are rejected in favor of a structural remedy that is purported to alone be sufficient to the task. The Catholic tradition affirms the need for a structural response to grave social challenges, but remains committed to the importance of spiritual practices, charitable forms of direct action, and structural responses to social crises.

In a sense, the argument made here is similar to Dorothy Day's observation, reviewed in Chapter 1, that the task of Catholics is to act not only when broad structural transformation is guaranteed, but *directly* here and now. We must begin to heal the earth in the most immediate and local manner possible. Wendell Berry, the noted farmer and poet from Kentucky, delineates what he takes to be the proper response to the environmental crisis:

> A lot of our smartest, most concerned people want to come up with a big solution to a big problem. I don't think that planet-saving, if we take it seriously, can furnish employment to many such people.... When I think of the kind of worker the job requires, I think of Dorothy Day (if one can think of Dorothy Day herself, separate from the publicity that came as a result of her rarity), a person willing to go down and down into the daunting, humbling, almost hopeless local presence of the problem—to face the great problem one small life at a time.[25]

Notably, this approach is endorsed by Francis in *Laudato Si'* when he invokes the little way of Saint Thérèse of Lisieux as the type of witness needed in an era of environmental degradation. He teaches: "Saint Thérèse of Lisieux invites us to practice the little way of love, not to miss out on a kind word, a smile or any small gesture which sows peace and friendship. An integral ecology is also made up of simple daily gestures which break with the logic of violence, exploitation and selfishness" (*LS*, 230). In this regard, a politics of mercy supports Francis's integral ecology, which calls for ecological conversion at the spiritual, individual, and local levels, an approach that will lead to sweeping social transformation.

Justice: Ecological Debt and the Moral Distribution of Goods

We end this book with the largest crisis we face. The other crises are, to a greater or lesser extent, global, but climate change quite literally envelops the globe. Francis's call for a bold cultural revolution applies most obviously and seriously to this crisis. The revolution he envisions would involve dramatic transformation of the economic and social status quo in each and every country on the planet. We write this book within the United States of America. Our country has an important role to play in responding to climate change and, we would hope, enacting the bold cultural revolution, not only because it has contributed disproportionately to climate change, but also because it still wields major geopolitical influence. We recognize that what we propose below regarding a structural approach to mercy may seem near impossible, but it is fully consistent with contemporary Catholic social teaching. The truly global crisis of climate change demands nothing short of a fundamental reconfiguration of our politics, economics, and civil society. We take this demand with grave seriousness and offer two structural remedies that respond to the ecological debt owed to the global poor.

Virtually every human being is complicit in the destruction of the environment in some way, but it is unambiguously the case that some persons and corporations bear more responsibility than others. Kate Aronoff makes this claim: "Just 100 companies have been responsible [for] over two-thirds of greenhouse gas emissions since the Industrial Revolution, and the richest 10 percent of people worldwide account for more than half of emissions from lifestyle choices."[26] Naomi Klein adds that fossil fuel companies have an enormous stake in the economy continuing to operate exactly as it does today (at 2014 market prices, fossil fuel in-the-ground reserves were worth $27 trillion).[27] There are many possible creative remedies to the ecological crisis. As we see it, a politics of mercy must include initiatives that address the affluent world's disproportionate responsibility for the crisis, which Francis calls **ecological debt**.

Francis believes that the affluent world (global North) owes the global poor (global South) some sort of reparations because of its disproportionate use of natural resources. He maintains that the prosperity that the global North enjoys also saddles it with a responsibility. Northern countries must limit consumption, curb emissions, and offer resources to poorer countries to support sustainable development. Francis admonishes: "We must continue to be aware that, regarding climate change, there are differentiated responsibilities" (*LS*, 52). This is an important claim, because the primary impediment to global climate treaties has been the refusal of affluent countries to take greater responsibility in reducing emissions.[28]

Because the natural resources of the earth disproportionality benefit the elite—in production as well as consumption—we should advocate for a mechanism that could more broadly distribute wealth generated from the goods of creation. Shortly after the publication of *Laudato Si'*, Francis declared in Bolivia: "The universal destination of goods is not a figure of speech found in the church's social teaching. It is a reality prior to private property. Property, especially when it affects natural resources, must always serve the needs of peoples."[29] While not dependent on Catholic social thought, Thomas Pogge has proposed a **global resource dividend** as a means of redressing the imbalances created by the global resource extraction and the consumption of natural resources. His proposal is very much consistent with Francis's claim about the universal destination of goods in relation to natural resources. The global poor rarely benefit from either resource extraction in their native lands (the wealth generated goes to national and global elites) or from the consumption of these resources (historically, the global North has been the primary beneficiary). Furthermore, because the global poor will be the population most adversely affected by the effects of climate change, it stands to reason that some compensatory mechanism should be created in order to remedy this situation. Pogge recommends a 1% resource dividend "based on the idea that the global poor own an inalienable stake in all limited natural resources."[30] It would be paid to a special fund any time a country decides to allow resources to be extracted from its land. Because the cost of this 1% dividend would be passed on to the consumer, it would ultimately amount to a "tax on consumption." The money collected from the global dividend would then be redistributed to the global poor, who have not reaped adequate benefit from the mechanisms of the current system. From the perspective of Catholic social teaching, this type of creative remedy follows quite logically from the universal destination of goods, insofar as it attempts to ensure that all human beings benefit from the goods of creation. A dividend on resource consumption would have the positive side effect of incentivizing a shift away from fossil fuels and toward more sustainable forms of energy consumption.

Obviously, both of these remedies demand the creation of an international regulatory and distributive body, since resources are widely distributed across national borders. Americans are often skeptical of international or transnational organizations, but they must notice that some already exist, such as the International Monetary Fund and the World Trade Organization, and that these wield enormous power to destroy the environment. *The Compendium of the Social Doctrine of the Catholic Church* argues:

> If it is true that everyone is born with the right to use the goods of the earth, it is likewise true that, in order to ensure that this right is exercised in an equitable and orderly fashion, regulated interventions are necessary, interventions that are the result of national and international agreements, and a juridical order that adjudicates and specifies the exercise of this right. (*CS*, 173)

As we noted in Chapter 1, Benedict XVI proposes in *Caritas in Veritate* that a global body be convened that would regulate international finance for the benefit of all. This proposal should be revisited and defended as a possible way of addressing ecological debt.[31]

Francis repeatedly remarks that *Laudato Si'* is directed toward all persons of good will (*LS*, 3 and 62). Its larger audience fits with the enormity of the climate crisis—a crisis similar to the nuclear arms race faced by John XXIII in *Pacem in Terris*, which also was addressed to all people of good will. Francis argues that because the reach of environmental destruction is global, it requires a global response, inclusive of religious and nonreligious communities. A diverse array of strategies should be employed to educate, to reform individual patterns of behavior and reduce consumption, to advocate for policy and structural reform at national and international levels, and to pursue an overarching politics rooted in the commitment to protecting our common home and its most vulnerable inhabitants. Francis framed our situation accurately: "if we destroy creation, creation will destroy us."[32] Even though the "us" in Francis's phrase certainly refers to all of humanity, we must not forget—and we cannot emphasize it enough—that lives sacrificed will number disproportionately among indigenous populations and the racialized urban poor, even as this crisis stems largely from the excesses of affluent populations in the global North (*LS*, 95). We must also remember the non-human species that suffer from this crisis, though they bear absolutely no responsibility for it. We owe them our care.

Conclusion: Bethlehem Farm

Bethlehem Farm is a Catholic intentional community located in Talcott, West Virginia. Its mission is to be "a Catholic community in Appalachia that transforms lives through service with the local community and the teaching of sustainable practices."[33] Each year the residential community at the farm welcomes more than 400 volunteers to join their practice of the four Gospel cornerstones of prayer, community, service, and simplicity, and then to bring the practice of these cornerstones back to their own homes so that they may change their own lifestyles and invite their neighbors to do the same. Bethlehem Farm was founded on the Feast of Mary's Immaculate Conception (December 8) in 2004 on the grounds of a former Catholic Worker farm. Since then it has operated as a community dedicated to putting on the mind of Christ (Phil 2:5–8) and living as a "contrast community" (a phrase borrowed from theologian Avery Cardinal Dulles) that functions, as Director Eric Fitts describes it, "to open eyes to the fact that there is another way to live" and "as a sign and symbol of the Christian life lived out."[34] Fitts recognizes that this contrast community is embedded in and interdependent with the surrounding community. Bethlehem Farm serves as a resource in contemplating the meaning of Christ's life, in living the works of mercy, and in caring for creation. Wider community members provide their resources: expertise in trades like plumbing and electrical; intimate knowledge of the local area, its history, and its land; and, of course, fellowship, whether through sharing faith or meals. Between these communities, everything connects.

Bethlehem Farm exemplifies a politics of mercy based on the corporal work of mercy of visiting the sick. It is a community dedicated to health and life, in many senses:

Spiritual health: Daily life on the farm is punctuated by prayer: at the day's beginning, before meals, before traveling out to worksites, at the day's end. The sacraments of Eucharist and Reconciliation are celebrated frequently, especially during the weeks when retreat groups visit. The main house on the farm has a chapel for Eucharistic adoration. And, with regard to the spiritual life in the sense of the life of the mind, visitors to the farm learn about sustainable practices and about structures of sin in our world (e.g., production, marketing, and sale of common items like clothing, which often involves sweatshop labor and massive water pollution; extraction, processing, and use of fossil fuels; waste management and mismanagement; and the use and abuse of water).

Bodily health of individuals: All who live at and visit the farm enjoy nutritious meals made from mostly local and organic ingredients. Farm life necessitates manual labor, from cultivating the yards and the vegetable garden and orchards, to caring for the chickens and donkeys, to maintaining farm buildings. And the farm's location in the forest-adorned West Virginia mountains allows opportunities for outdoor recreation such as hiking and, in the valleys, swimming in ponds and the Greenbrier River.

Communal health: Farm community members and visitors work with members of the wider community to repair homes and to cultivate farms. Such collaboration provides the opportunity to share stories, community meals (members of the wider community have a standing invitation to attend a community meal at the farm on Tuesday evenings), and interfaith fellowship (Catholics from Bethlehem Farm regularly attend Bible study at a local Protestant church). Bethlehem Farm residents often join others from the local area at protests of corporate and state abuses of the local community. As an example, they have joined local resistance to the building of the Mountain Valley Pipeline, which passes roughly a mile downhill from Bethlehem Farm.

Creation's health: Distinctive to Bethlehem Farm's mission is its focus on sustainability, especially with the recent construction of the San Damiano Center for Sustainability in 2019. Bethlehem Farm cultivates the earth with organic farming, care for animals, composting (including composting toilets), simplicity (minimizing waste, and water and electric use), renewable energy (solar power and hot water), and by fostering a way of life marked by periods of time dedicated to appreciating nature and meditating on the mountains, meadows, and streams—and the God who made them.

A refrain at Bethlehem Farm is "Welcome home!" Visitors are greeted with these words, both on the sign at the end of the driveway and by the caretakers who engage them as they arrive. After a day at a work site, the crew that returns is welcomed home by those who stayed back at the farm. The phrase "welcome home" echoes God's mercy, particularly as Jesus depicts it in his parables and in his life. "Welcome home" characterizes the reception of the prodigal son by his magnanimous father (Lk 15:11–32). "Welcome home" fits with Jesus's words to the repentant criminal on the cross, "Today you will be with me in paradise" (Lk 23:43). "Welcome home" resonates with the promise of land that God made to Abram (Gen 15:18–21), which will be fulfilled in an ultimate way in the New Jerusalem (Rev 21:1–22:5). But here and now, "Welcome home" propels a politics of mercy that originates in communities like Bethlehem Farm that hear the cry of the poor and the cry of the earth. West Virginia is a land of those who tend to be forgotten in a globalized, business-centered economy; a land ravaged by drug addiction and hopelessness; a land increasingly torn by clear-cutting of forests, mountaintop removal mining, pollution of water, and collapsing of land through fracking; and the destruction of habitat for numerous animal species. It is a land riven by multiple forms of violence. But so, too, is West Virginia a land of creativity, skill, and kinship; a land of lush green vegetation; breathtaking mountaintop views; flowing creeks, streams, and rivers that bring freshness to the land and joy to the people; the howls of coyotes, the songs of birds, the majesty of deer—and the stars, more than the sands on the beach, glimmering in a black sky unsullied by city lights. It is a land where peace can and does spring forth. In West Virginia, even as it cries out in supplication, creation, human and beyond, gives glory to God. Christ's deep incarnation reverberates. The Gospel is being lived. Healing is coming. Welcome to our common home!

Notes

1   Geophysical Fluid Dynamics Laboratory (Princeton University), "Global Warming and Hurricanes: An Overview of Current Research Results," https://www.gfdl.noaa.gov/global-warming-and-hurricanes/.

2   Emily Atkin, "Florida's Poop Nightmare Has Come True," *The New Republic*, September 14, 2017, https://newrepublic.com/article/144798/floridas-poop-nightmare-come-true.

3   Justin Worland, "Why We Won't Be Ready for the Next Hurricane Harvey Either," *Time*, August 28, 2017, http://time.com/4919224/hurricane-harvey-houston-policy/.

4   Amanda Holpuch and Oliver Laughland, "Puerto Rico: Trump Appears to Complain about Cost of Relief Effort," *The Guardian*, October 23, 2017, https://www.theguardian.com/world/2017/oct/03/puerto-rico-donald-trump-visit-hurricane-maria.

5   Katherine Burton, Rebecca Spalding, and Michelle Kaske, "Maria Made Puerto Rico's Giant Debt Even Trickier for Hedge Funds," *Bloomberg Businessweek*, October 12, 2017, https://www.bloomberg.com/news/articles/2017-10-12/maria-made-puerto-rico-s-giant-debt-even-trickier-for-hedge-funds.

6   David Wallace-Wells, "The Uninhabitable Earth," *New York Magazine*, July 10, 2017, http://nymag.com/intelligencer/2017/07/climate-change-earth-too-hot-for-humans.html.

7   David Wallace-Wells, *The Uninhabitable Earth: Life after Warming* (New York: Tim Duggan Books, 2019), 2.

8   Wallace-Wells, "The Uninhabitable Earth."

9   Dana Nuccitelli, "Is the Climate Consensus 97%, 99.9%, or Is Plate Tectonics a Hoax?" *The Guardian*, May 3, 2017, https://www.theguardian.com/environment/climate-consensus-97-per-cent/2017/may/03/is-the-climate-consensus-97-999-or-is-plate-tectonics-a-hoax.

10 Naomi Oreskes and Erik Conway, *Merchants of Doubt: How a Handful of Scientists Obscured the Truth on Issues from Tobacco Smoke to Global Warming* (New York: Bloomsbury Publishing, 2011).

11 Bryan Massingale, "Katrina Catastrophe Exposes U.S. Race Reality," *National Catholic Reporter*, March 2, 2007.

12 Kanta Kumari Rigaud, Alex de Sherbinin, Bryan Jones, Jonas Bergmann, Viviane Clement, Kayly Ober, Jacob Schewe, Susana Adamo, Brent McCusker, Silke Heuser, and Amelia Midgley, *Groundswell: Preparing for Internal Climate Migration*, World Bank, Washington, DC, 2018, https://openknowledge.worldbank.org/handle/10986/29461.

13 Kate Yoder, "US Military Emits More CO_2," *Grist*, June 12, 2019, https://grist.org/article/u-s-military-emits-more-co2-than-most-countries/.

14 Pope Paul VI, *Octogesima adveniens*, May 14, 1971, https://w2.vatican.va/content/paul-vi/en/apost_letters/documents/hf_p-vi_apl_19710514_octogesima-adveniens.html; idem, "Message of His Holiness Paul VI to Mr. Maurice F. Strong, Secretary-General of the Conference on the Environment," June 1, 1972, https://w2.vatican.va/content/paul-vi/en/messages/pont-messages/documents/hf_p-vi_mess_19720605_conferenza-ambiente.html.

15   Pope John Paul II, "Peace with God the Creator, Peace with All of Creation: Message of His Holiness Pope John Paul II for the Celebration of the World Day of Peace (1 January 1990)," December 8, 1989, https://w2.vatican.va/content/john-paul-ii/en/messages/peace/documents/hf_jp-ii_mes_19891208_xxiii-world-day-for-peace.html, 6–7.

16   John Paul II, "Peace with God," 8.

17   Benedict XVI, "Message of His Holiness for World Day of Peace," https://w2.vatican.va/content/benedict-xvi/en/messages/peace/documents/hf_ben-xvi_mes_20091208_xliii-world-day-peace.html.

18   Niels Henrik Gregersen, "The Cross of Christ in an Evolutionary World," *Dialog* 40, no. 3 (Fall 2001): 192–207.

19   Elizabeth A. Johnson, *Creation and the Cross: The Mercy of God for a Planet in Peril* (Maryknoll, NY: Orbis Books, 2018), 184–85.

20   Denis Edwards, *Deep Incarnation: God's Redemptive Suffering with Creatures* (Maryknoll, NY: Orbis Books, 2019).

21   Johnson, *Creation and the Cross*, 185–86.

22   Johnson, *Creation and the Cross*, 193.

23   Pope Francis, "Letter of His Holiness Pope Francis for the Establishment of the 'World Day of Prayer for the Care of Creation,'" August 6, 2015, http://w2.vatican.va/content/francesco/en/letters/2015/documents/papa-francesco_20150806_lettera-giornata-cura-creato.html.

24   Pope Francis, "Message of His Holiness Pope Francis for the Celebration of the World Day of Prayer for the Care of Creation," September 1, 2016, http://w2.vatican.va/content/francesco/en/messages/pont-messages/2016/documents/papa-francesco_20160901_messaggio-giornata-cura-creato.html#_ftn9. The following quotations are from this same message.

25   Wendell Berry, *Sex, Economy, Freedom & Community: Eight Essays* (New York: Pantheon, 1993), 25.

26   Kate Aronoff, "Denial by a Different Name." *Intercept*, April 17, 2018. https://theintercept.com/2018/04/17/climate-change-denial-trump-germany/.   See also Tess Riley, "Just 100 Companies Responsible for 71% of Global Emissions,

Study Says," *The Guardian*, July 10, 2017. https://www.theguardian.com/sustainable-business/2017/jul/10/100-fossil-fuel-companies-investors-responsible-71-global-emissions-cdp-study-climate-change.

27 Naomi Klein, *This Changes Everything: Capitalism vs. the Climate* (New York: Simon and Schuster, 2015), 129.

28 Fiona Harvey and Ben Doherty, "China Demands Developed Countries 'Pay Their Debts' on Climate Change," *The Guardian*, December 13, 2018, https://www.theguardian.com/science/2018/dec/13/china-demands-developed-countries-pay-their-debts-on-climate-change.

29 Thomas Pogge, *World Poverty and Human Rights: Cosmopolitan Responsibilities and Reforms* (New York: Polity, 2008), 202.

30 Thomas Pogge, "An Egalitarian Law of Peoples," *Philosophy and Public Affairs* 23, no. 3 (1994): 195–224, 220.

31 *The Catechism of the Catholic Church* notes that "political authority has the right and duty to regulate the legitimate exercise of the right to ownership for the sake of the common good" (*CC*, 2406), http://www.vatican.va/archive/ccc_css/archive/catechism/p3s2c2a7.htm.

32 Cindy Wooden, "Destroying Creation Is Destroying a Gift of God, Pope Says at Audience," CNS News, May 21, 2014. http://www.catholicnews.com/services/englishnews/2014/destroying-creation-is-destroying-a-gift-of-god-pope-says-at-audience.cfm.

33 For more information, see Bethlehem Farm's website: http://bethlehemfarm.net/.

34 Email communication with Eric Fitts, September 14, 2019.

T HIS BOOK PRESENTS AN apologetic for the Catholic faith in an era
marked by the loss of confidence in the institutional church as a
result of the sexual abuse and other crises. Why remain Catholic? A
major reason is that we see mercy embodied in the world through
Catholic organizations and communities like the Catholic Worker,
Jesuit Refugee Service, Homeboy Industries, Catholic Relief Services,
and Bethlehem Farm.

The Catholic approach to mercy is distinctive among today's political alternatives. We have argued in this book that a Catholic politics of
mercy entails spiritual practices, charitable works, and an attempt to
build structures of justice in society. There certainly are other spiritu-
alities out there. There certainly are other philanthropic networks that
promote charity. There are other proponents of a structural remedy to
the challenges that we face. But a Catholic politics of mercy, which is
not just a theoretical possibility (found in books like this one!) but also
the lived experience of Catholic communities, brings these elements
together in a powerful and unique way.

The politics of mercy is of particular relevance in this moment, as
we watch a number of interconnected crises unfold before us. Pope
Francis's statement in *Laudato Si'* that "everything is connected" is a
timely message in view of the challenges of inequality, racism, and
violence described in this book. The crises we have analyzed are rarely
treated together. Likewise, the local and the global are rarely treated in
the same breath. We have done both of those things here.

We have examined between this book's two covers the varied yet
interspersed crises of wealth inequality, lack of solidarity toward
migrants, mass incarceration, war, and climate change. We have done
so by featuring vastly different Catholic communities that address
these crises at a grassroots, yet often global, level.

Bethlehem Farm is the most "local" of our examples. With this
community, we have a group of people in West Virginia attempting

to heal a relatively small parcel of land and community. They do this, though, with an eye to the global range of the environmental crisis and crises that intersect with it, among them wealth inequality and war.

Jesuit Refugee Service is the most "global" of our examples. This organization has vast range. It works to build a more inclusive and reconciled social order in 56 countries around the world. The service does this, though, with an eye to the inalienable dignity of each and every person it serves. And like Bethlehem Farm, it sees the crisis over solidarity with migrants as linked to environmental destruction, war, incarceration, and inequality.

We have taken the approach we have because we are Catholic. "Catholic" means, we say once more, "universal." A Catholic approach is a holistic one. It must take into account the spiritual, the material, the local, the global, and every step and link between them. It does this because of the church's faith in Christ, the face of God's mercy, who reconciles *all things* to himself, whether in heaven or on earth (Col 1:20).

The parable of the Last Judgment is the only place in the Gospels where Jesus tells us how we will be judged: "Amen, I say to you, whatever you did (not do) for one of these least brothers of mine, you did (not do) for me.... [The accursed] will go off to eternal punishment, but the righteous to eternal life" (Mt 25:40, 45–46). Throughout the Catholic tradition, this parable has been taken as a sign of hope. Of course, there is the threat of eternal punishment, but more important to notice is the opportunity to which this parable points. By feeding the hungry, giving drink to the thirsty, welcoming the stranger, clothing the naked, caring for the sick, and visiting the prisoner, we literally encounter Christ among us. The poor, those marginalized with respect to race, and those who fall victim to violence are "the least of these" today. Those who perform the works of mercy, through spiritual practices, charitable actions, and building structures of justice and peace, will join the communion of the saints and will enjoy the fruits of the resurrection. That is the promise. This is our faith. This is the reason for our hope.

BIBLIOGRAPHY

Ahern, Kevin. "The Justice Legacy of *Populorum Progressio*: A Jesuit Case Study." *Journal of Moral Theology* 6, no. 1 (2017): 39–56.

———. *Structures of Grace: Catholic Organizations Serving the Common Good*. Maryknoll, NY: Orbis Books, 2015.

Alexander, Michelle. *The New Jim Crow: Mass Incarceration in the Age of Colorblindness*. New York: New Press, 2012.

Alison, James. *Raising Abel: The Recovery of the Eschatological Imagination*. New York: Crossroad-Herder, 1996.

Amadeo, Kimberly. "U.S. Military Budget." *The Balance*, April 22, 2019. https://www.thebalance.com/u-s-military-budget-components-challenges-growth-3306320.

Anderson, Gary. *Charity: The Place of the Poor in the Biblical Tradition*. New Haven, CT: Yale University Press, 2013.

Appleby, Scott. *The Ambivalence of the Sacred: Religion, Violence, and Reconciliation*. Lanham, MD: Rowman & Littlefield, 2000.

Aronoff, Kate. "Denial by a Different Name." *Intercept*, April 17, 2018. https://theintercept.com/2018/04/17/climate-change-denial-trump-germany/.

Arrupe, Pedro, SJ. "The Society of Jesus and the Refugee Problem" [Letter to all Major Jesuit Superiors]. November 14, 1980. http://www.jrsusa.org/Assets/Sections/Downloads/ArrupeLetter.pdf.

Atkin, Emily. "Florida's Poop Nightmare Has Come True." *The New Republic*, September 14, 2017. https://newrepublic.com/article/144798/floridas-poop-nightmare-come-true.

Bacevich, Andrew J. *American Empire: The Realities and Consequences of U.S. Diplomacy*. Cambridge, MA: Harvard University Press, 2002.

Bauman, Michelle. "Twenty Years after Genocide, Church Helps Rwanda Heal." *Catholic News Agency*, April 7, 2014. https://www.catholicnewsagency.com/news/twenty-years-after-rwandan-genocide-church-helps-bring-healing.

Baxter, Michael. "Just War and Pacifism: A 'Pacifist' Perspective in Seven Points." *Houston Catholic Worker Newsletter*, June 1, 2004. https://cjd.org/2004/06/01/just-war-and-pacifism-a-pacifist-perspective-in-seven-points/.

Benedict XVI [Joseph Ratzinger]. *Caritas in Veritate*. June 29, 2009. http://w2.vatican.va/content/benedict-xvi/en/encyclicals/documents/hf_ben-xvi_enc_20090629_caritas-in-veritate.html.

———. *Deus Caritas Est*. December 25, 2005. http://w2.vatican.va/content/benedict-xvi/en/encyclicals/documents/hf_ben-xvi_enc_20051225_deus-caritas-est.html.

———. "Message of His Holiness for World Day of Peace." https://w2.vatican.va/content/benedict-xvi/en/messages/peace/documents/hf_ben-xvi_mes_20091208_xliii-world-day-peace.html.

———. *Spe Salvi*. November 30, 2007. http://w2.vatican.va/content/benedict-xvi/en/encyclicals/documents/hf_ben-xvi_enc_20071130_spe-salvi.html.

———. *Values in a Time of Upheaval*. San Francisco: Ignatius Press, 2006.

Benedict of Nursia. *The Rule of St. Benedict*. Edited by Timothy Frye, Timothy Horner, and Imogene Baker. Collegeville, MN: Liturgical Press, 1981.

Berry, Wendell. *Sex, Economy, Freedom & Community: Eight Essays*. New York: Pantheon, 1993.

Boyle, Gregory. *Barking to the Choir: The Power of Radical Kinship*. New York: Simon & Schuster, 2017.

———. *Tattoos on the Heart: The Power of Boundless Compassion*. New York: Simon & Schuster, 2010.

Brooks, Arthur. "Confessions of a Catholic Convert to Capitalism." *America*, February 6, 2017. https://www.americamagazine.org/politics-society/2017/02/06/confessions-catholic-convert-capitalism.

Burke, Jason. "Mukesh Ambani, India's Richest Man, Builds World's First Billion-Dollar Home." *The Guardian*, October 13, 2010. https://www.theguardian.com/world/2010/oct/13/mukesh-ambani-india-home-mumbai.

Burton, Katherine, Rebecca Spalding, and Michelle Kaske. "Maria Made Puerto Rico's Giant Debt Even Trickier for Hedge Funds." *Bloomberg Businessweek*, October 12, 2017. https://www.bloomberg.com/news/articles/2017-10-12/maria-made-puerto-rico-s-giant-debt-even-trickier-for-hedge-funds.

Cacho, Lisa Marie. *Social Death: Racialized Rightlessness and the Criminalization of the Unprotected*. New York: New York University Press, 2012.

Cahill, Lisa Sowle. *Blessed Are the Peacemakers: Pacifism, Just War, and Peacebuilding*. Minneapolis, MN: Fortress Press, 2019.

Cakebread, Caroline, and Katie Warren. "Jeff Bezos Is Dropping $80 Million." *Business Insider*, June 4, 2019. https://www.businessinsider.com/jeff-bezos-owns-five-massive-homes-across-the-united-states-2017-10.

Camp, Jordan T. *Incarcerating the Crisis: Freedom Struggles and the Rise of the Neoliberal State*. Oakland: University of California Press, 2017.

Chomsky, Aviva. *They Take Our Jobs! And 20 Other Myths about Immigration*. Boston, MA: Beacon Press, 2018.

Coles, Robert. *Dorothy Day: A Radical Devotion*. Reading, MA: Perseus, 1987.

Consedine, Jim. "Faith and the Financial Crisis." *Houston Catholic Worker* 29, no. 1 (January–February 2009). https://cjd.org/2009/02/01/faith-and-the-financial-crisis/.

Cupich, Cardinal Blase. "Witnessing to a Consistent Ethic of Solidarity." *Commonweal*, May 19, 2017. https://www.commonwealmagazine.org/cardinal-blase-cupich-signs-times.

Day, Dorothy. *The Long Loneliness*. New York: Harper & Row, 1952; repr. 1997.

———. "More about Holy Poverty, Which Is Voluntary Poverty." *The Catholic Worker* (February 1945), 1–2.

———. *Selected Writings: By Little and By Little*. Maryknoll, NY: Orbis Books, 2005.

Dear, John. "The Catholic Campaign to End Iraq War." *National Catholic Reporter*, August 21, 2017. https://www.ncronline.org/blogs/road-peace/catholic-campaign-end-iraq-war.

Edwards, Denis. *Deep Incarnation: God's Redemptive Suffering with Creatures*. Maryknoll, NY: Orbis Books, 2019.

Fontaine, Richard. "The Nonintervention Delusion." *Foreign Affairs*, November/December 2019. https://www.foreignaffairs.com/articles/2019-10-15/nonintervention-delusion.

Francis, Pope [Jorge Mario Bergoglio]. "Address of His Holiness Pope Francis to Participants in the Third World Meeting of Popular Movements," November 5, 2016. http://w2.vatican.va/content/francesco/en/speeches/2016/november/documents/papa-francesco_20161105_movimenti-popolari.html.

———. "Address of the Holy Father (Kangemi Slum in Nairobi, Kenya)." November 27, 2015. http://w2.vatican.va/content/francesco/en/speeches/2015/november/documents/papa-francesco_20151127_kenya-kangemi.html.

——. "Address of the Holy Father (Meeting with Representatives of Civil Society, Paraguay)," July 11, 2015. https://w2.vatican.va/content/francesco/en/speeches/2015/july/documents/papa-francesco_20150711_paraguay-societa-civile.html.

——. "Address of the Holy Father (Second World Meeting of Popular Movements, Bolivia)," July 9, 2015. http://w2.vatican.va/content/francesco/en/speeches/2015/july/documents/papa-francesco_20150709_bolivia-movimenti-popolari.html.

——. "Address of the Holy Father (Visit to Curran-Fromhold Correctional Facility)," September 27, 2015. http://w2.vatican.va/content/francesco/en/speeches/2015/september/documents/papa-francesco_20150927_usa-detenuti.html.

——. "Address of the Holy Father to 'Astalli Centre,'" September 9, 2013. http://w2.vatican.va/content/francesco/en/speeches/2013/september/documents/papa-francesco_20130910_centro-astalli.html.

——. "Address to the New Non-Resident Ambassadors to the Holy See: Kyrgyzstan, Antigua and Barbuda, Luxembourg, and Botswana," May 16, 2013. http://w2.vatican.va/content/francesco/en/speeches/2013/may/documents/papa-francesco_20130516_nuovi-ambasciatori.html.

——. "Address to Participants in the International Forum on 'Migration and Peace,'" February 21, 2017. http://w2.vatican.va/content/francesco/en/speeches/2017/february/documents/papa-francesco_20170221_forum-migrazioni-pace.html.

——. "Angelus." July 10, 2016. https://w2.vatican.va/content/francesco/en/angelus/2016/documents/papa-francesco_angelus_20160710.html.

——. "A Big Heart Open to God: An Interview with Pope Francis." Interviewed by Antonio Spadaro, SJ. *America*, September 30, 2013. https://www.americamagazine.org/faith/2013/09/30/big-heart-open-god-interview-pope-francis.

——. *Evangelii Gaudium*. November 24, 2013. http://w2.vatican.va/content/francesco/en/apost_exhortations/documents/papa-francesco_esortazione-ap_20131124_evangelii-gaudium.html.

——. "General Audience." June 5, 2013. https://w2.vatican.va/content/francesco/en/audiences/2013/documents/papa-francesco_20130605_udienza-generale.html.

——. *Laudato Si'*. May 24, 2015. http://w2.vatican.va/content/francesco/en/encyclicals/documents/papa-francesco_20150524_enciclica-laudato-si.html.

——. "Letter of His Holiness Pope Francis for the Establishment of the 'World Day of Prayer for the Care of Creation,'" August 6, 2015. http://w2.vatican.va/content/francesco/en/letters/2015/documents/papa-francesco_20150806_lettera-giornata-cura-creato.html.

——. "Message of His Holiness Pope Francis for the Fiftieth World Day of Peace," January 1, 2017. https://w2.vatican.va/content/francesco/en/messages/peace/documents/papa-francesco_20161208_messaggio-l-giornata-mondiale-pace-2017.html#_ftnref15.

——. "Message of His Holiness on World Day of Prayer for the Care of Creation," September 1, 2016. http://w2.vatican.va/content/francesco/en/messages/pont-messages/2016/documents/papa-francesco_20160901_messaggio-giornata-cura-creato.html.

——. "Message on the Occasion of the 35th Anniversary of the Centro Astalli," April 19, 2016. https://w2.vatican.va/content/francesco/en/messages/pont-messages/2016/documents/papa-francesco_20160419_videomessaggio-centro-astalli-35anniv.html.

——. "Te Deum Homily," May 25, 2003. http://www.arzbaires.org.ar/inicio/homilias/homilias2003.htm#Tedeum25/5/2003.

——. "Vigil of Prayer for Peace," September 7, 2013. http://www.vatican.va/content/francesco/en/homilies/2013/documents/papa-francesco_20130907_veglia-pace.html.

——. "Visit to the Penitentiary (Cereso N. 3) of Ciudad Juárez," February 26, 2016. https://w2.vatican.va/content/francesco/en/speeches/2016/february/documents/papa-francesco_20160217_messico-detenuti.html.

Galtung, John. "Cultural Violence." *Journal of Peace Research* 27, no. 3 (August 1990): 291–305.

Garcia, Adrian. "Most Americans Wouldn't Cover a 1K Emergency with Savings." *Bankrate*, January 16, 2019. https://www.bankrate.com/banking/savings/financial-security-january-2019/.

Geophysical Fluid Dynamics Laboratory (Princeton University), 2018. "Global Warming and Hurricanes: An Overview of Current Research Results." https://www.gfdl.noaa.gov/global-warming-and-hurricanes/.

Golash-Boza, Tanya. *Deported: Immigrant Policing, Disposable Labor, and Global Capitalism*. New York: New York University Press, 2015.

——. "The Parallels between Mass Incarceration and Mass Deportation: An Intersectional Analysis of State Repression." *Journal of World Systems Research* 22, no. 2 (2016): 484–509.

Gregersen, Niels Henrik. "The Cross of Christ in an Evolutionary World." *Dialog* 40, no. 3 (Fall 2001): 192–207.

Hartford Catholic Worker. "We Are the Hartford Catholic Worker." Video. https://hartfordcatholicworker.org/our-history/.

Harvey, Fiona, and Ben Doherty. "China Demands Developed Countries 'Pay Their Debts' on Climate Change." *The Guardian*, December 13, 2018. https://www.theguardian.com/science/2018/dec/13/china-demands-developed-countries-pay-their-debts-on-climate-change.

Headley, William R., and Reina C. Neufeldt. "Catholic Relief Services: Catholic Peacebuilding in Practice." In *Peacebuilding: Catholic Theology, Ethics, and Praxis*, edited by Robert Schreiter, Scott Appleby, and Gerard Powers. Maryknoll, NY: Orbis Books, 2010, 125–154.

Holpuch, Amanda, and Oliver Laughland. "Puerto Rico: Trump Appears to Complain about Cost of Relief Effort." *The Guardian*, October 23, 2017. https://www.theguardian.com/world/2017/oct/03/puerto-rico-donald-trump-visit-hurricane-maria.

Hussain, Murtaza. "It's Time for America to Reckon with the Staggering Death Toll of the Post-9/11 Wars." *The Intercept*, November 19, 2018. https://theintercept.com/2018/11/19/civilian-casualties-us-war-on-terror/.

Johnson, Elizabeth A. *Creation and the Cross: The Mercy of God for a Planet in Peril*. Maryknoll, NY: Orbis Books, 2018.

Keenan, James F. *The Works of Mercy: The Heart of Catholicism*. Lanham, MD: Rowman & Littlefield, 2017.

Kelly, Stephanie. "U.S. Spending on Prisons Grew at Three Times Rate of School Spending: Report." *Reuters*, July 27, 2016. https://www.reuters.com/article/us-usa-education-funding-idUSKCN0ZN2L2.

Khazan, Olga. "Most Prisoners Are Mentally Ill." *The Atlantic*, April 7, 2015. https://www.theatlantic.com/health/archive/2015/04/more-than-half-of-prisoners-are-mentally-ill/389682/.

Kinzer, Stephen. *Overthrow: America's Century of Regime from Hawaii to Iraq*. New York: Times Books, 2007.

Klein, Naomi. *This Changes Everything: Capitalism vs. the Climate*. New York: Simon and Schuster, 2014.

Kolvenbach, Peter-Hans. "Review of the Jesuit Refugee Service." A Letter to the Society of Jesus, February 14, 1990.

Korgen, Jeffrey Odell. "Forgiveness Unbound: Reconciliation Education Is Helping Rwanda to Heal." *America*, September 10, 2007. https://www.americamagazine.org/issue/624/article/forgiveness-unbound.

Jaffe, Ina. "Cases Show Disparity of California's Three Strikes Law," *National Public Radio*, October 30, 2009. https://www.npr.org/templates/story/story. php?storyId=114301025.

Jesuit Refugee Service. "Advocacy." https://jrs.net/en/programme/advocacy/.

———. "The Charter of Jesuit Refugee Service." https://jrsap.org/Assets/Sections/ Downloads/char-en21.pdf.

———. "JRS—2018 Annual Report." https://jrs.net/wp-content/uploads/2019/06/ JRS-2018-annual-report.pdf.

———. "Our Impact." https://jrs.net/en/our-work/our-impact/.

Jesuit Refugee Service East Africa. "Accompaniment." http://www.jrsea.org/ accompaniment.

Jesuit Refugee Service Europe. "I Get You." https://jrseurope.org/assets/Regions/ EUR/media/files/JRS_Europe_igetyou_full.pdf.

John XXIII. *Pacem in Terris*. April 11, 1963. http://www.vatican.va/content/john-xxiii/en/encyclicals/documents/hf_j-xxiii_enc_11041963_pacem.html.

John Paul II [Karol Wojtyla]. (Promulgated). *Catechism of the Catholic Church*. 1992. http://www.vatican.va/archive/ENG0015/_INDEX.HTM.

———. *Evangelium Vitae*. March 25, 1995. http://www.vatican.va/content/john-paul-ii/en/encyclicals/documents/hf_jp-ii_enc_25031995_evangelium-vitae. html.

———. *Laborem Exercens*. September 14, 1981. http://w2.vatican.va/content/john-paul-ii/en/encyclicals/documents/hf_jp-ii_enc_14091981_laborem-exercens. html.

———. "Peace with God the Creator, Peace with All of Creation." December 8, 1989. http://w2.vatican.va/content/john-paul-ii/en/messages/peace/documents/ hf_jp-ii_mes_19891208_xxiii-world-day-for-peace.html.

Johnson, Elizabeth A. *Creation and the Cross: The Mercy of God for a Planet in Peril*. Maryknoll, NY: Orbis Books, 2018.

Lajoie, Ron. "To Forgive: Rwanda Two Decades after the Genocide." *Catholic New York*, November 13, 2013. http://cny.org/stories/to-forgive-rwanda-two-decades-after-the-genocide,10219.

The Land Report. "The Land Report 100." https://www.landreport.com/americas-100-largest-landowners/.

Lind, Dara. "The Disastrous, Forgotten 1996 Law that Created Today's Immigration Problem." *Vox*, April 28, 2016. https://www.vox.com/2016/4/28/11515132/iirira-clinton-immigration.

Lloyd, Vincent. "Prisons Are a Biblical Abomination." *Church Life Journal*, February 26, 2019. https://churchlifejournal.nd.edu/articles/prisons-are-a-biblical-abomination/.

Lopez, Ian Hanley. *Dog Whistle Politics: How Coded Racial Appeals Have Reinvented Racism and Wrecked the Middle Class*. New York: Oxford University Press, 2015.

Macais, Amanda. "America Has Spent 6.4 Trillion on Wars in the Middle East and Asia." CNBC, November 20, 2019. https://www.cnbc.com/2019/11/20/us-spent-6point4-trillion-on-middle-east-wars-since-2001-study.html.

Magno, Paul. "The Plowshares Anti-Nuclear Movement at 35: A Next Generation?" *Bulletin of the Atomic Scientists* 72, no. 2 (2016): 85–88.

Massingale, Bryan. "Katrina Catastrophe Exposes U.S. Race Reality." *National Catholic Reporter*, March 2, 2007.

———. *Racial Justice and the Catholic Church*. Maryknoll, NY: Orbis Books, 2010.

Moberg, Benjamin. "A Mandatory Mistake." *Sojourners*, February 19, 2015. https://sojo.net/articles/mandatory-mistake.

Nakamura, David. "Trump Administration Moving Quickly to Build Up Nationwide Deportation Force." *Washington Post*, April 12, 2017. https://www.washingtonpost.com/politics/trump-administration-moving-quickly-to-build-up-nationwide-deportation-force/2017/04/12/7a7f59c2-1f87-11e7-be2a-3a1fb24d4671_story.html.

National Center for Children. "Child Poverty." http://www.nccp.org/topics/child-poverty.html.

Nixon, Rob. *Slow Violence and the Environmentalism of the Poor*. Cambridge, MA: Harvard University Press, 2011.

Nuccitelli, Dana. "Is the Climate Consensus 97%, 99.9%, or Is Plate Tectonics a Hoax?" *The Guardian*. May 3, 2017. https://www.theguardian.com/environment/climate-consensus-97-per-cent/2017/may/03/is-the-climate-consensus-97-999-or-is-plate-tectonics-a-hoax.

O'Brien, Kevin. "Consolation in Action: The Jesuit Refugee Service and the Ministry of Accompaniment." *Studies in Jesuit Spirituality* 37, no. 4 (2015): 1–51.

Oreskes, Naomi, and Erik Conway. *Merchants of Doubt: How a Handful of Scientists Obscured the Truth on Issues from Tobacco Smoke to Global Warming*. New York: Bloomsbury Publishing, 2011.

Oxfam International. "Five Shocking Facts about Extreme Global Inequality." https://www.oxfam.org/en/5-shocking-facts-about-extreme-global-inequality-and-how-even-it.

Patterson, Orlando. *Slavery and Social Death: A Comparative Study*. Cambridge, MA: Harvard University Press, 1982.

Paul VI, Pope. "Day of Peace," January 1, 1972. http://w2.vatican.va/content/paul-vi/en/messages/peace/documents/hf_p-vi_mes_19711208_v-world-day-for-peace.html.

———. "Message of His Holiness Paul VI to Mr. Maurice F. Strong, Secretary-General of the Conference on the Environment," June 1, 1972. https://w2.vatican.va/content/paul-vi/en/messages/pont-messages/documents/hf_p-vi_mess_19720605_conferenza-ambiente.html.

———. "Message of His Holiness Paul VI for the Observance of a Day of Peace," January 1, 1968. http://w2.vatican.va/content/paul-vi/en/messages/peace/documents/hf_p-vi_mes_19671208_i-world-day-for-peace.html.

———. [Giovanni Battista Enrico Antonio Maria Montini]. *Octogesima Adveniens*, May 14, 1971. https://w2.vatican.va/content/paul-vi/en/apost_letters/documents/hf_p-vi_apl_19710514_octogesima-adveniens.html.

Pendelton, Devon. "World's Richest Lose 117 Billion." August 5, 2019. https://www.bloomberg.com/news/articles/2019-08-05/world-s-richest-lose-117-billion-in-one-day-market-meltdown.

Phan, Peter C. "*Deus Migrator*—God the Migrant: Migration of Theology and Theology of Migration." *Theological Studies* 77, no. 4 (2016): 845–68.

Pimentel, Diego Alejo Vázquez, Iñigo Macías Aymar, and Max Lawson. "Reward Work, Not Wealth." Oxfam International, January 22, 2018. https://www-cdn.oxfam.org/s3fs-public/file_attachments/bp-reward-work-not-wealth-220118-summ-en.pdf.

Pogge, Thomas. "An Egalitarian Law of Peoples." *Philosophy and Public Affairs* 23, no. 3 (1994): 195–224.

———. *World Poverty and Human Rights: Cosmopolitan Responsibilities and Reforms*. New York: Polity, 2008.

Price, Joshua. *Prison and Social Death*. New Brunswick, NJ: Rutgers University Press, 2015.

Pursuing Just Peace. Edited by Mark M. Rogers, Tom Barnat, and Julie Ideh. Baltimore, MD: Catholic Relief Services, 2008.

Reese, Thomas. "Jesuit Refugee Service: Accompanying, Serving, Advocating." *National Catholic Reporter*, October 6, 2016. https://www.ncronline.org/blogs/faith-and-justice/jrs-accompanying-serving-and-advocating-refugees.

Rigaud, Kanta Kumari, Alex de Sherbinin, Bryan Jones, et al. *Groundswell: Preparing for Internal Climate Migration*. Washington, DC: The World Bank, 2018.

Roy, Arundhati. *Capitalism: A Ghost Story*. New York: Haymarket Books, 2014.

Sacchetti, Maria. "ICE Chief Tells Lawmakers Agency Needs Much More Money for Immigration Arrests." *Washington Post*, June 13, 2017, https://www.washingtonpost.com/local/social-issues/ice-chief-tells-lawmakers-agency-needs-much-more-money-for-immigration-arrests/2017/06/13/86651e86-5054-11e7-b064-828ba60fbb98_story.html.

Schlabach, Gerald. "Just War? Enough Already." *Commonweal*, May 31, 2017. https://www.commonwealmagazine.org/just-war-0.

Second Vatican Council. *Gaudium et Spes*. http://www.vatican.va/archive/hist_councils/ii_vatican_council/documents/vat-ii_const_19651207_gaudium-et-spes_en.html.

Singh, Nikhil Pal. *Race and America's Long War*. Oakland: University of California Press, 2017.

Slater, Alice. "The US Has Military Bases in 80 Countries." *The Nation*, January 24, 2018. https://www.thenation.com/article/archive/the-us-has-military-bases-in-172-countries-all-of-them-must-close/.

Stillman, Sarah. "Lampedusa's Migrant Tragedy, and Ours." *The New Yorker*, October 10, 2013. https://www.newyorker.com/news/daily-comment/lampedusas-migrant-tragedy-and-ours.

Tweed, David. "China Defense Spending Set to Rise." *Bloomberg*, March 4, 2019. https://www.bloomberg.com/news/articles/2019-03-05/china-s-military-spending-slows-as-economy-cools.

UN-Habitat. *The Challenge of Slums: Global Report on Human Settlements*. Sterling, VA: Earthscan Publications, 2003.

U.S. Conference of Catholic Bishops. *Open Wide Our* Hearts. November 2018. http://www.usccb.org/issues-and-action/human-life-and-dignity/racism/upload/open-wide-our-hearts.pdf.

U. S. Conference of Catholic Bishops. *Responsibility, Rehabilitation, and Restoration: A Catholic Perspective on Crime and Criminal Justice*. November 15, 2000. http://

www.usccb.org/issues-and-action/human-life-and-dignity/criminal-justice-restorative-justice/crime-and-criminal-justice.cfm#policy.

U.S. Department of Housing and Urban Development. "The 2018 Annual Homeless Assessment Report." December 2018. https://files.hudexchange.info/resources/documents/2018-AHAR-Part-1.pdf.

Vatican News. "Pope at Mass: Be Free from Fear of Migrants and Refugees." *Vatican News*, February 2019. https://www.vaticannews.va/en/pope/news/2019-02/pope-francis-mass-sacrofano-migrants-refugees.html.

———. "Pope Saddened by Death." *Vatican News*, June 2019. https://www.vaticannews.va/en/pope/news/2019-06/pope-sorrow-death-migrants-death-united-states-mexico-border.html.

Wallace-Wells, David. "The Uninhabitable Earth." *New York Magazine*, July 10, 2017. http://nymag.com/intelligencer/2017/07/climate-change-earth-too-hot-for-humans.html.

———. *The Uninhabitable Earth: Life after Warming.* New York: Tim Duggan Books, 2019.

Weber, Kerry. "Shadowed by Tragedy: Rwanda Strives to Rise above a History of Horror." *America*, April 7, 2014. https://www.americamagazine.org/issue/shadowed-tragedy#.

Weigel, George. "The Catholic Difference: Getting 'Just-War' Straight." *Zenit*, October 13, 2001. https://zenit.org/articles/george-weigel-on-just-war-principles/.

Weisbrot, Mark, Stephan Lefebvre, and Joseph Sammut, "Did NAFTA Help Mexico?: An Assessment After 20 Years." Center for Economic and Policy Research, February 2014.

Woo, Carolyn. "Blessed Are the Peacemakers." *Catholic Relief Services*, https://www.crs.org/media-center/carolyn-woo%E2%80%99s-cns-column-blessed-are-peacemakers.

Wooden, Cindy. "Destroying Creation Is Destroying a Gift of God, Pope Says at Audience." *CNS News*, May 21, 2014. http://www.catholicnews.com/services/englishnews/2014/destroying-creation-is-destroying-a-gift-of-god-pope-says-at-audience.cfm

———. "Pope Francis on Prison Systems: 'We will be judged on this.'" *America*, November 8, 2019. https://www.americamagazine.org/politics-society/2019/11/08/pope-francis-prison-systems-we-will-be-judged.

Worland, Justin. "Why We Won't Be Ready for the Next Hurricane Harvey Either." *Time*, August 28, 2017. http://time.com/4919224/hurricane-harvey-houston-policy/.

Yoder, Kate. "U.S. Military Emits More CO_2." *Grist*, June 12, 2019. https://grist.org/article/u-s-military-emits-more-co2-than-most-countries/.